Software Wasteland

How the Application-Centric Mindset is Hobbling our Enterprises

Dave McComb

Technics Publications

Published by:

2 Lindsley Road
Basking Ridge, NJ 07920 USA
https://www.TechnicsPub.com

Edited by Lauren McCafferty
Cover design by Lorena Molinari

First Printing 2018

Copyright © 2018 by Dave McComb

ISBN, print ed.	9781634623162
ISBN, Kindle ed.	9781634623179
ISBN, ePub ed.	9781634623186
ISBN, PDF ed.	9781634623193

Library of Congress Control Number: 2017964492

Dedicated to Heidi for her patience during the long gestation of this manuscript.

Contents

Introduction

Enterprise IT (Information Technology) is a $3.8 trillion per year industry worldwide, and $1 trillion in the US alone.[1] The Enterprise IT industry is twice the size of the world petroleum industry.[2] Capital spending for IT in the US is now $700 billion per year.[3] At 32% of the total capital spend, it exceeds construction and is closing in on equipment spending. At least half – and perhaps as much as three fourths – of this spending is wasted. The capabilities that are delivered fall far short of what our technology makes possible.

We (and by "we," I refer to the people in charge of estimating, proposing, and executing information

---

[1] See Appendix for details.

[2] http://bit.ly/2fmMrY4.

[3] http://bit.ly/2kKGtrC.

application projects or system integration projects) have come to simply accept the current state. It has become the norm to have projects cost tens of millions, hundreds of millions, or even billions of dollars, and routinely run over budget and schedule by hundreds of percent. These budget and monetary "overages" are almost all waste. However, the waste is hard to see, after being so marbled through all the products, processes, and guiding principles. That is where this book comes in. We must see, understand, and agree about the problem before we can take coordinated action to address it.

We refer to the current state of affairs as "the Application-Centric Quagmire." Our root cause analysis, detailed in Chapter 3, pins the industries' current woes on a firmly entrenched mindset, which we call being "Application-Centric." We watch firms addicted to this mindset struggle to break free. But struggling to free yourself, while still clinging to the beliefs that keep you stuck is not a solution. We've come to refer to this situation as the "quagmire" because after decades of watching executives struggle with their systems, it seems apt. The harder they flail and the more they invest, the more stuck they become.

Not everyone has the problems described in this book. A few firms (mostly those that were founded in the 21st century, often called the "digital natives") have managed to avoid the quagmire. Avoiding the quagmire is how Instagram managed to scale to 100 million users with a team of five building, deploying, and managing their apps. Amazon pushes changes to its systems up to five times a second. They are not in the quagmire.

Most established companies are well enmeshed in the quagmire. Moreover, failing to understand the behavior and mindsets that got them in the quagmire will keep them stuck. This book is for the companies that are frustrated with their current systems, and suspect that things could be much, much better.

The trajectory of this book is as follows:

- In Chapter 1, we explore how bad the current state is. We're talking about waste at a terrific scale.

- In Chapter 2, we explore the economics of the software industry. Many of the lessons we've brought across from other industries don't apply here. Additionally, the economic tradeoffs are changing at the speed of Moore's Law, but our approaches are not keeping pace.

- In Chapter 3, we use "root cause analysis" to reveal the real contributors to this situation.

- Chapter 4 recounts the many attempts we've made in the past to deal with information system complexity, and why they have been marginally effective.

- Chapter 5 dismantles seven fallacies that sound good on the surface, but contribute to our remaining stuck.

- The quagmire is not affecting all sectors of the economy equally. Chapter 6 looks at how this is playing out in the government and private sectors, large and small companies, and various parts of the IT industry itself.

- Chapter 7 outlines some action you can take now to begin to extricate yourself.

This book is intentionally bleak. It is intended to get you sufficiently riled up to take action. Chapter 7 provides some immediate actions you can take to stop the pain. The companion book is where we propose a longer-term fix and a way to stay away from quagmires permanently.

Throughout this book when I use the pronouns "we" or "our", I am usually referring to experience that I or my associates at Semantic Arts have found and concur on, from 18 years of helping large firms tackle these issues. When I say "I", I refer to personal observations that may not be as widely held.

CHAPTER 1
How bad is it?

In this section, we will put some parameters on the size of the problem. These estimates may seem extreme on first reading, but in reality, what you read here is most likely an understatement.

WASTE IN THE INFORMATION SYSTEMS INDUSTRY

Lean manufacturing and the Toyota Production Systems have dramatically improved productivity and quality in the physical goods industries. Enterprise IT has barely scratched the surface. This book is about examining how rampant waste has crept into our industry.

We can learn a lot from the many decades wherein Lean manufacturing has been systematically examining and removing waste from manufacturing processes. What I like about Lean (and the reason it applies well to the information systems industry) is that practitioners become rabid to seek out, identify, and eliminate waste. We have so much to learn.

As Ohno Taiicho put it:

> *Waste is anything other than the minimum amount of equipment, materials, parts, and working time which is absolutely essential to add value to the product or services.*

Lean separates waste into three main sources:

- Mura (unevenness)
- Muri (overburden)
- Muda (activities that do not add value)

Muda is what most people think of when they think of Lean. Muda contains these "seven wastes" per Ohno Taiicho:

- Transport
- Inventory
- Motion
- Waiting
- Over-Processing
- Overproduction
- Defects

To this list of the original seven wastes, some people also add the following:

- Talent

- Resources
- By-Products

It is tempting to try to make a direct analogy between manufacturing and software production and implementation, but this is a poor analogy. Manufacturing creates physical goods from raw materials and other resources. However, the creation of a new software artifact from an existing one (via copying) is practically free. When you download the latest version of Linux, the only charge is a bit of network connectivity. In the physical world, even making a bad knock-off of a product consumes resources and entails the possibility of quality mishaps.

This isn't to say that there isn't waste in software implementation, but we need to explore the nature of software economics (which we will do in Chapter 2) before we can have a more detailed discussion of waste in information systems.

Later in this section, we will make a macro estimate of the degree of waste possible in the enterprise IT industry. First, though, we'll examine three important sub-sectors of the industry.

INDUSTRIES THAT CLEAN UP THE WASTE

There are whole industries specializing in cleaning up some of the more egregious bits of waste. Within the umbrella, three sub-industries are generally recognized:

- Legacy Software Industry
- Neo-Legacy Software Industry
- Legacy Modernization Industry

LEGACY SOFTWARE INDUSTRY

I had the misfortune of being on a project that probably bore the last non-pejorative use of the term "legacy" in connection with a software project. I helped build a five-year strategic information plan for Johns Manville Corporation in 1990. We believed this plan would leave a legacy for the sponsors, and accordingly named it the "Legacy Plan." Shortly after, the monolithic mainframe programs that everyone had and no one could get rid of became known collectively as "legacy systems." No one advertises themselves as being in the legacy software industry, but many are. Hacker Rank estimates there are 220 billion lines of Cobol code in production, with 1.5 billion more added every year.[4]

Two things make a legacy system the albatross that everyone disdains. First is that it is built in languages or databases that are no longer supported. The other is that changing a legacy system is cost-prohibitive. A surprisingly large percentage of newly implemented systems are still expensive and difficult to change. In this day and age, there is no excuse for this. What we have instead are reputations, habits, and perverse incentives.

---

[4] http://bit.ly/2AoL9KJ.

Reputation comes into play when customers want to deal with established companies. The software vendor who entered the market first is often the most established with the largest installed base and most customers. They also have the oldest architecture.

Habit comes in on the buyer and seller side. Software developers and implementers are most comfortable with what they have had the most experience with using. The more senior (and typically decision-making) developers are often most comfortable with the oldest technology, and will revert to their comfort zone.

Vinnie Mirchandani's excellent book, *SAP Nation*,[5] describes how the SAP ecosystem has become addicted to complexity, and how SAP's various attempts to rein it in have been mostly rebuffed by the firms that make a living at implementing it.

NEO-LEGACY SOFTWARE INDUSTRY

> *... In so doing, they are creating the legacy systems of the future.*

Malcolm Chisholm[6]

> *The legacy systems of tomorrow are being written today.*

Martin Fowler[7]

---

[5] http://amzn.to/2iFFdRY.

[6] Managing Reference Data in Enterprise Databases, Malcolm Chisholm, Morgan Kaufman, 2001 p281.

Just as no one claims to be in the legacy software industry, no one claims to be in the neo-legacy industry. The neo-legacy industry is what Martin Fowler was talking about (20 years ago!).

Almost the entire enterprise application software industry is neo-legacy. How to spot a neo-legacy application:

- High cost of making simple changes
- Added cost to integrate with other systems
- Future data migrations are baked in

Most of this book is about understanding how our attitude toward application software is setting the stage for us to create problems faster than we solve them.

LEGACY MODERNIZATION INDUSTRY

The legacy modernization industry is the only one of the three that will admit to being in a legacy industry. It is relatively small, and is composed of companies that specialize in converting client groups away from their legacy environments. Sometimes, they are converting clients to a neo-legacy environment, but often it is a step in the right direction.

There are legacy-understanding companies, whose roles are to help firms understand either what is hidden in their legacy code, or what is hidden in their legacy data.

---

[7] Martin Fowler, in a presentation mid 1990s.

Then there are legacy conversion companies. Most find ways to emulate legacy code in modern languages, or legacy data structures in modern databases.

Both are often necessary. Often the legacy conversion companies can get a company off a "burning platform" in a short amount of time, and buy time to make a further conversion. A "burning platform" is one where a parent company or agency has announced it will no longer support a language, database, operating system, or hardware line; or that a vendor has gone out of business and therefore the product can no longer be supported; or it has become impossible to find the skills to continue to support the product.

The legacy conversion often isn't the end stage. However, compared to a rewrite or package implementation that might take five to ten years, a conversion that leaves you with the same functionality (often with lower licensing costs) is attractive.

However, the legacy understanding sub-industry may be more important. We have watched legacy conversions stall out, either due to internal sabotage (the incumbents do not want their monopoly on understanding to be undermined) or sheer conservatism (we just don't know what else may break). These backfires could be avoided if the sponsors of the conversion had been armed with complete definitive information about what was in the legacy system.

The deep secret is that the legacy system has very few important business rules, and a lot of special logic devoted to conditions that are no longer of interest to the sponsoring organization.

A THOUGHT EXPERIMENT ON WASTE

If we wanted to get a handle on the overall level of waste in the transportation industry (and thereby get a handle on the size of the opportunity that awaits its solution), we might do something like the following (for just the personal terrestrial commute sub-market):

- Inventory of the number of trips consumers make in their cars, buses, and trains each year

- Add up the total capital costs invested in supporting this (all the cars, trains, roads, and rails)

- Add up all the operating costs (fuel, tires, maintenance)

- Then calculate the average cost per trip

- Next create a model of what the cost per trip could be (assume as ride sharing has demonstrated that private automobiles could go from 5% utilization to 75%+, and that the whole gas guzzling fleet is swapped for electric vehicles)

If you did this exercise, I predict that you would conclude that at least half of the $2 trillion we currently have is waste – or to put it another way, opportunity. This is exactly the sort of disruption currently being ushered in by the ride-sharing and autonomous vehicle industry.

The economics in the software industry are so much more extreme.

Because the software industry has no physicality, and the cost to replicate code or data is close to zero, the potential savings are staggering. If you observe closely, you will see that most of the software industry consists of writing the same application code over and over again, in different contexts, to different data models and in different computer languages.

Our construction analogy falls apart here. Building the same house over and over again makes sense, because everyone can't live in the same house. But we can, in principle, run our companies on a limited amount of code. It's not as simple as it first sounds, but it is possible.

Business application systems only perform a few dozen different functions. These functions may include displaying a field on a form, validating a field, detecting a particular change in a value, and sending a message. Many people think that sending an email is a different function from sending a text message, or that detecting that an account balance is overdue is different from detecting that an inventory item has reached its reorder point. However, these are not different functions; they are merely parametric differences of the same function being applied.

Building a system is a matter of design (what types of data to store, what processes to employ, how to package functionality into useable interactions, etc.) and implementation is a matter of supplying the parametric settings to each of the functions needed to implement the system.

How much code does the world need? The logical answer is "just enough." We need enough code to implement those few functions, plus some infrastructure to hold it all together, as well as some code that will adapt all the various bits of hardware linked with these systems. This includes the Internet of Things (IoT), which will need adapters for all the sensors and actuators that can be attached to the IoT.

But we only need one copy of each, which could be copied and cached where needed for performance reason.

The entire application software industry could conceivably become a $0 billion industry, with what little remains to be done is professional services designing and configuring more appropriate systems for each company and potentially each employee and citizen.

A large enterprise with over $1 billion in annual IT spend should create a vision for the long-term economics of its information system infrastructure. Once you understand where the dis-economy lays, it is not that hard to conceive of a future free from waste, at a fraction of the current spend.

This will take time.

While it is just a thought experiment, it is already beginning to happen. As we will discuss later in this book, the spread of cloud computing is dropping the cost of hardware and making the cost of licensing software more noticeable. By using open source operating systems such as Linux, and open source databases such as Postgres, firms are escaping the burden of paying licenses per use. Moreover, Linux and Postgres are examples of something that only had to be written once and widely distributed.

The application software industry is currently far from this state. The few open source options for application software packages that exist are pretty bad knockoffs of the current neo legacy offerings. However, all this is poised to change.

Sometimes to understand pathology, it helps to look at some of the most extreme forms. For that, we will look at some examples of projects that have spent 100 to 1000 times more than even current technology would suggest is necessary, and taking my earlier thought experiment to its extreme, on the order of 10,000 times more than it potentially could cost.

HOW TO SPEND A BILLION DOLLARS ON A MILLION-DOLLAR SYSTEM

Social scientists and economists are dismayed by the difficulty in performing controlled studies. While there is no shortage of hypothesis about human behavior or complex systems, it is often too expensive or unethical to set up and execute true side-by-side controlled studies. Nevertheless, every now and then the world serves up "natural experiments." A natural experiment occurs where, by coincidence, most of the features of a controlled experiment happen spontaneously.

One of my favorites is the hypothesis that a market driven, capitalist society would provide higher degrees of prosperity than a socialist or communist economic system. Most studies that attempt to demonstrate this are pure correlations. We can correlate GDP with key features of the economic model, but this strategy risks confounding cause and effect: perhaps the more affluent choose market economics, rather than the market economy driving affluence.

What is needed is a controlled experiment. In a controlled experiment for this hypothesis, you would take a population that is as similar as possible. Many people believe that certain ethnic or cultural groups have advantages in professions that benefit from market economies. So ideally, you would like a population as ethnically and culturally homogenous as possible.

Many people believe that economic prosperity comes largely from access to resources, such as land, minerals, or oil. So if your experiment divided the two study groups, each would be given similar natural resources and similar access to trade routes, ports, or navigable waters.

There are obvious differences between individual people, and many economic truths are complex systems requiring the interplay of thousands of organizations and individuals. Individuals, groups, and organizations need to be able to freely enter and exit various roles in the economy. For an experiment to be truly valid, it would need to involve millions of people. This is one of the reasons that experiments of this type are so rarely performed.

Finally, these differences don't manifest overnight. It would be preferable to run the experiment for decades, or better yet, for generations. The barriers to conducting such an experiment are immense. Nevertheless, every now and then, circumstances serve up all the prerequisites.

After World War II, the Korean Peninsula (which had been occupied by Japan during the war) was temporarily partitioned. The north was aligned with Communist China and Russia, and the south was with the west—especially the United States. From 1950 to 1953, the forces of the west and east clashed in the Korean peninsula. At various times in the war each side seemed to be close to complete victory, but in the end after massive loss an armistice was signed, and the country was partitioned along the 38th parallel.

North Korea and South Korea at the time were populated with homogenous populations with similar ethnic and cultural backgrounds and similar work ethics. The two landmasses were similar in size and had similar access to natural resources and harbors.

The primarily difference between the "control group" in the north, and the "experimental group" in the south, was the south adopted the Western model of democracy, market economy, and capitalism. The experiment has now run for over 60 years. To underscore the need to run an experiment over an economy you need to be patient. For the first twenty years of the experiment, the differences were relatively small. However, small differences compounded over time result in extreme differences.

We could use statistics to make the point (and the statistics are compelling[8]) but the difference is so stark that it can be seen from space (courtesy NASA). In the following satellite picture taken at night, Japan is the crescent shape on the right, with Tokyo the bright spot on the right edge. The lights in the upper left corner are part of Liaoning Province in China. The bright light on the left and the lights around it are Seoul and the rest of

---

[8] http://bit.ly/2h5PIxZ.

South Korea. If you didn't know otherwise, you might think that the dark area between South Korea and Liaoning Province was water, as there are just a few pinpricks of light that might be fishing trawlers.

But not so. That region (20% larger than South Korea) is the nearly lightless North Korea.

I bring this up to suggest that sometimes the world serves up natural experiments that are so much more compelling than reams of correlations or pontifications, that we should recognize them when we see them and take the learnings to heart.

A TALE OF TWO PROJECTS

If someone has a $100 million project, the last thing that would occur to them would be to launch a second project in parallel using different methods to see which method works better. That would seem to be insane, almost asking for the price to be doubled. Besides, most sponsors of projects believe they know the best way to run such a project.

However, setting up and running such a competition would establish once and for all what processes work best for large scale application implementations. There would be some logistical issues to be sure, but well worth it. To the best of my knowledge, though, this hasn't happened.

Thankfully, the next best thing *has* happened. Luckily, we have recently encountered a "natural experiment" in the world of enterprise application development and deployment. We are going to mine this natural experiment for as much as we can.

President Barack Obama signed the Affordable Care Act into law in March 23, 2010. The project was awarded to CGI Federal, a division of the Canadian company, CGI, for $93.7 million. I'm always amused at the spurious precision the extra $0.7 million implies. It sort of signals that somebody knows exactly how much this project is going to cost. It is just the end product of some byzantine negotiating process. It was slated to go live October 2013. (I was blissfully unaware of this for the entire three years the project was in development).

One day in October 2013, one of my developers came into my office and told me he had just heard of an application system comprising over 500,000,000 lines of code. He couldn't fathom what you would need 500,000,000 lines of code to do. He was a recent college graduate, had been working for us for several years, and had written a few thousand lines of elegant architectural code. We were running major parts of our company on these few thousand lines of code so he was understandably puzzled at what this could be.

We sat down at my monitor and said, "Let's see if we can work out what they are doing."

This was the original, much maligned rollout of Healthcare.gov. We were one of the few that first week who managed to log in and try our luck (99% of the people who tried to access healthcare.gov in its first two weeks were unable to complete a session).

As each screen came up, I'd say "what do you think this screen is doing behind the scenes?" and we would postulate, guess a bit as to what else it might be doing, and jot down notes on the effort to recreate this. For instance, on the screen when we entered our fake address (our first run was aborted when we entered a Colorado address as Colorado was doing a state exchange) we said, "What would it take to write address validation software?" This was easy, as he had just built an address validation routine for our software.

After we completed the very torturous process, we compiled our list of how much code would be needed to recreate something similar. We settled on perhaps tens of thousands of lines of code (if we were especially verbose). But no way in the world was there any evidence in the functionality of the system that there was a need for 500,000,000 lines of code.

Meanwhile news was leaking that the original $93 million project had now ballooned to $500 million.

In the following month, I had a chance encounter with the CEO of Top Coder, a firm that organizes the equivalent of X prizes for difficult computer programming challenges. We discussed Healthcare.gov. My contention was that this was not the half-billion dollar project that it had already become, but was likely closer to the coding challenges that Top Coder specialized in. We agreed that this would make for a good Top Coder project and began looking for a sponsor.

Life imitates art, and shortly after this exchange, we came across HealthSherpa.com. The Health Sherpa User Experience was a joy compared to Healthcare.gov. I was more interested in the small team that had rebuilt the equivalent for a fraction (a tiny fraction) of the cost.

From what I could tell from a few published papers, a small team of three to four in two to three months had built equivalent functionality to that which hundreds of professionals had spent years laboring over. This isn't exactly equivalent. It was much better in some ways, and fell a bit short in a few others.

In the ensuing years, I'd used this as a case study of what is possible in the world of enterprise (or larger) applications. Over the course of the ensuing four years,

I've been tracking both sides of this natural experiment from afar.

I looked on in horror to watch the train wreck of the early rollout of Healthcare.org balloon from $1/2 billion to $1 billion (many firms have declared victory in "fixing" the failed install for a mere incremental $1/2 billion), and more recently to $2.1 billion. By the 2015 enrolment period, Healthcare.gov had adopted the HealthSherpa user experience, which they now call "Marketplace lite." Meanwhile HealthSherpa persists, having enrolled over 800,000 members, and at times handles 5% of the traffic for the ACA.

The writing of this book prompted me to research deeper, in order to crisp up this natural experiment playing out in front of us. I interviewed George Kalogeropoulos, CEO of HealthSherpa, several times in 2017, and have reviewed all the available public documentation for Healthcare.gov and HealthSherpa.

The natural experiment that has played out here is around the hypothesis that there are application development and deployment process that can change the resource consumption and costs by a factor of 1,000. As with the Korean Peninsula, you can nominate either side to be the control group. In the Korea example, we could say that communism was the control group and market democracy the experiment. The hypothesis would be that the experiment would lead to increased prosperity. Alternatively, you could pose it the other way around: market democracy is the control and dictatorial communism is the experiment that leads to reduced prosperity.

If we say that spending a billion dollars for a simple system is the norm (which it often is these days) then that becomes the control group, and agile development becomes the experiment. The hypothesis is that adopting agile principles can improve productivity by many orders of magnitude. In many settings, the agile solution is not the total solution, but in this one (as we will see), it was sufficient.

This is not an isolated example – it is just one of the best side-by-side comparisons. What follows is more evidence that application development and implementation are far from waste-free.

CANADIAN FIREARMS

A program to register firearms in Canada was originally projected to have a net cost of $2 million. The actual write-up was that it would cost $119 million to develop and garner $117 in net new revenue – a couple of curiously precise estimates.

The real cost was $2 billion.[9] They have registered 5.6 million firearms. This is a textbook example of "this was way harder than we thought." Except that there is no reason it should have been. There is nothing inherently

---

[9] http://bit.ly/1LXhDq2.

complex about registering guns. You have to work at it to make it complex enough to spend $2 billion of someone else's money.

SPORTING GOODS MANUFACTURER

There is a $2 billion sporting goods manufacturer that has two main product lines. Within each product line, they have thousands of products. In 2007, they embarked on a project to replace their aging systems with a state-of-the-art ERP system. Enterprise Resource Planning systems, as we'll discuss in Chapters 2 and 3, are integrated packaged software systems meant to cover a large percentage of a firm's functionality. The ERP system chosen was one of the top three mid-tier systems. They had the best help to implement the system.

They went live in 2015. Total project costs over the 8-year period are estimated to be approximately $50 million. This was considered a success, but the point I'd like to make in this book is that most of this cost and time was driven from the tools and approaches that are accepted to be best practice now. In the companion book we describe a future state where implementing a system such as this would be a $1 or $2 million project, taking about a year, with much less risk.

INSURANCE CONGLOMERATE

We have reviewed the 10Ks of an insurance conglomerate and confirmed the story we were told.

A certain company (which shall remain nameless, as they have mostly managed to avoid publicity) decided to employ a major systems integrator to help them "integrate" the many companies they had acquired. Seemed like a good idea.

Somehow, the project rather than seek early small wins, decided to go for the big integrated solution. Bummer. After $250 million invested, nothing was implemented and the subsidiaries are as unintegrated as they ever were.

MAJOR BANK

We have become privy to the story of a major bank that opted for a project that was going to implement all their systems in a "big bang" integrated project implementation.

Incredibly, they spent $1 billion before cancelling the project (and before implementing anything). It is hard to figure out what is more incredible: 1) that a publically held company could spend a billion dollars on a failed experiment and keep it out of the news or 2) that it didn't occur to anyone to do something incremental along the way.

DIMHRS

The Department of Defense in 2006 launched into a project to consolidate their many human resource systems into one. They chose to base the new system on packaged software (see Chapter 5 for why this is a mistake).

They cancelled the project after spending a billion dollars and realized they had virtually nothing implemented.

CANCER RESEARCH INSTITUTE

There is a cancer research institute that got involved in a major initiative that cost them $63 million before they pulled the plug with nothing to show for it.

Summary

One of the lessons here is this: organize your projects such that every few million dollars or so, you could cancel the project and still have something to show for it. A $60 million project should have thrown off many interim implementations each worth more than the investment to date.

You may scoff at the many bad systems implementation projects, but that is to be expected, given the number of projects being executed every day.

Yes, these are the extreme cases. But these wouldn't have occurred if the norm were to build these systems using agile methods and composition from reusable parts. In order to get these extreme cases, the norm has to be in a very abnormal place.

As of this writing, the norm for "large" system implementation projects is:

- Initial budget $100 million
- Initial time frame 3-5 years
- Cancellation rate 50%
- The "successful" projects are typically 50%-100% over budget and years over schedule

If that is the norm, then yes, a few will run over by 1000%, just as a few bad apples will spoil the bunch.

The point of this book is that that should not be the norm. All those apples are bad.

By the way, if you make your living selling or implementing these bloated systems, you should probably just throw this book down now. It will only make you angry.

> *"It is difficult to get a man to understand something when his salary depends on his not understanding it."*[10]
>
> Upton Sinclair

If you are on the buying side of the equation, this book could change the way you think of systems.

---

[10] http://bit.ly/2jALTIA.

CHAPTER 2
The hidden levers driving waste

The overruns and waste described in the last section are real. I have watched some of these projects. This is not embezzlement or accounting fraud. This is a lot of well-meaning people working very hard to complete difficult tasks.

What we want to explore in this section is what people are inadvertently doing that is running up the costs. In Chapter 4, we look at some entrenched beliefs that keep this diseconomy locked in, but first we need to understand what is going on.

HOW TO THINK ABOUT INFORMATION SYSTEMS RESOURCES

Costs in information systems do not behave as they do in more tangible industries, and attempts to apply analogies from one area to the other are fraught with misapplication.

Traditional industries have been viewed through a lens based on the nature and relative amount of resource types they consume. The most common being:

- Material
- Labor
- Capital
- Energy

Traditional agriculture was labor- and capital-intensive (the capital being the land). Modern agriculture is capital and energy intensive, as the amount of labor per unit of output has plummeted, the resource consumption taking its place being machinery and fuel.

The information systems industry has a slightly different set of drivers.

The cost of an information system, ultimately, is the resources consumed to create and run it. There are many intermediary players in this industry, and many different pricing models, but ultimately the resources consumed must be paid for. If a vendor of a subscription-based application manages to charge significantly more for an annual subscription that the resources they consume, they will make outsized profits for a while. But these margins will attract new players to the niche. Eventually the subscription cost will be driven down by competition to closer to the resource costs. For this reason we focus our analysis on the resource costs, which over the long run will be the real drivers, even though some short-term profit making will occur.

Let's look at the main categories of resource consumption and how they behave economically. The main categories of how costs are incurred are:

- Computer hardware
- Networking costs
- Software licenses
- Professional services

You can likely think of many more categories, but they are subsumed by these. For instance, Software as a Service (SaaS) is a bundling of hardware, networking, and software licensing costs that are charged in a different manner but underneath they consume those resources. We shall return to some of the common bundlings after we describe these four in a bit more detail.

COMPUTER HARDWARE

At one point, CPUs and storage devices dominated the cost of an information system. In the 1950's a mainframe computer cost tens of millions of dollars. There were no networking costs and what little software there was came with the implementation. A small team of analysts took care of the design and programming of the systems.

Since then, the cost of a transistor has been falling at an impressive rate, dropping well over a billion fold over 40 years.[11]

Six decades of Moore's law have seen the capacity of our hardware explode, while the cost has plummeted to near zero. One hardware component, disk drive space, dropped 100,000 fold over 29 years.[12]

The cost of storage has come down even more impressively. In 30 years, the cost for one megabyte of storage has gone from $250,000 to 3 cents.

Many of us making decisions about computer systems learned our basic design tradeoffs and habits at a time when the cost of storage was a million times higher than it is now. Many of the architectures we base our systems on were likewise built at a time when hardware costs ruled the world.

We marvel that the processing power of the smart phone in your pocket exceeds that of the mission control computers that sent the first men to the moon. Yet the reality is even more extreme than that. The computer in your pocket cost several hundred dollars. Commodity

---

[11] http://bit.ly/2kkYjNE.

[12] http://bit.ly/1FPdGS.

chips, such as those that power the myriad devices in our cars or appliances, can be acquired for as little as one cent, and with 50,000 transistors running at 20 million instructions per second, they are roughly equivalent to the ground control computers for the Apollo Moon Mission.

The total amount spent on computer hardware per year is still a huge number ($1 trillion) but the amount of computer hardware needed for any given application is no longer the significant part of the equation.

We still need computer hardware to run our systems, but the cost is hardly a factor anymore, and we will need to rethink how we trade hardware costs for other costs.

NETWORKING COSTS

The computer network, which we use to transfer data, voice, and video, is of course largely hardware-based as well. Most people separate networks and communication from processing and storage hardware expenses, due at least in part because the network became an externalized outside utility.

The proprietary data networks of the 1960's and 1970's, such as SNA from IBM and DECNet from Digital Equipment, have all the same disadvantages of today's non-interchangeable proprietary "lock in" platforms. With the advent of open standards such as Ethernet and TCP/IP, new entrants could compete at any layer in the communication stack and performance and efficiency blossomed.

Over thirty years we've seen about a 100,000-fold improvement in internet throughput and speed.[13]

For many years, processing and storage were relatively cheap, and communicating between computers was relatively expensive and slow. We developed strategies that accommodated these tradeoffs. We updated databases on a weekly or monthly basis with small streams of transactions that shuttled the changes from one system to another. We often had dedicated communication links to allow piping data from system to system in uninterrupted bursts.

Message based architectures, with Service-Oriented Architecture being the most mature, were developed to organize the transfer of small transactions from the system that created a change to others that needed to know about the change. We developed the idea that data could be packaged into messages and sent from queue to queue. Industries have become organized around standards for messaging such as HL7 in healthcare, ACORD in Insurance, SIP in telecommunication, and EDI in retail.

Then once the World Wide Web took hold, what seemed unthinkable just a few decades prior became

---

[13] http://bit.ly/2nRkpg6.

commonplace. The idea that a transaction or a file might be exploded into dozens of "packets" and sent in different routes, usually being forwarded between dozens of network nodes, each owned and controlled by different organizations, and arriving at its destination a few hundred milliseconds after it was sent, went from fantasy to reality.

The revenue models of the World Wide Web rewarded suppliers that could increase bandwidth and decrease latency. In the 1980's, Nicholas Negroponte of the MIT Media lab observed the evolution of the telephone and the television marketplaces. In an almost comical historical accident, each marketplace selected the delivery technology that would have much better suited the other. Telephony was using delivery technology that was really better suited for television, and vice versa.

Telephone was our connection to the home and office network. In the one hundred years leading up to the 1980's, AT&T had run a string of copper to virtually every establishment in the United States, and other telecoms had done the same overseas. Meanwhile, radio and television, being later to the game, had the option of using what at the time were scarce radio frequencies.

So we had a telephone network tethered to the land by the copper wires that carried their signals, at a time when it was becoming apparent that the near future would want telecommunication to be portable (as opposed to being tied to your home or office). At the same time, televisions, which were still large and not portable, would benefit from the higher bandwidth of fixed cable, and had little to lose in giving up portability.

The "Negroponte Switch" was the observation that we had all the network capacity we needed—it was just poorly assigned. If we ran TV over the phone lines and gave the phone companies the broadcast TV airwaves, everyone would be happy. Nevertheless, logistically, this type of "switch" just couldn't happen. Not only was there no way to seize all those assets and reallocate them, the number of devices that would have to be swapped out simultaneously and repurposed was mind-boggling. So for some time, the Negroponte Switch was just a paradox. We knew what was needed, but there was no route to get us there.

There is no evidence that Negroponte foresaw the developments that would allow his switch to become reality. The cable TV industry was born around this time, and rather than repurpose the phone network that AT&T had spent a century to build, the wildcatters of the early cable industry managed to lay a cable to everyone's home in a matter of a decade or two.

Meanwhile, with the invention of the cell phone, the United States government was convinced to free up previously unavailable spectra that had been set aside for military use. The cellular phone industry planted cell towers every few miles across the country. Where there had been two major communication networks, now there were four. In a matter of a bit more than a decade, the Negroponte switch had become affected. Within a couple of decades the copper wires to "land line" phones and the TV broadcast channel airwaves would both become obsolete.

Networks and communication costs are generally metered in one way or another. We pay for throughput (how many bits we shipped from one location to another) and often a premium for speed. There are many billing arrangement options. For instance, cell phone carriers generally charged a fixed amount up to a particular throughput (in the case of a cell phone, download and upload traffic), but we are still essentially paying for the movement of a given amount of data.

For many information systems, the concept of "latency" in communication is more important than the communication capacity. A low latency network is one where you can get a response very rapidly. For a long time, latency in a computer application was managed by having computer terminals talking to a tuned database at the other end. As long as the database could serve up a response in less than a couple of seconds, the network rarely added more than a half a second and the user had an acceptable experience.

In the 1980's and early 1990's, data communication on common carriers was comically slow by today's standards. A dial up acoustic modem would deliver 300 to 2400 bits per second. With error correction, most characters are 10 bits, and therefore this speed was 30 to 240 characters per second. This is scarcely faster than a skilled typist. It is no wonder that systems and architectures built in this era assumed relatively fast connections to local databases, which were synched up asynchronously.

We can now rapidly and economically transmit volumes of data that a few decades ago would have been more rapidly transferred by loading tapes on to a 747 and flying them to their destination.

SOFTWARE LICENSES

Software is intellectual property, with a high one-time capital cost, but a near zero cost to replicate. In the absence of a license fee, the cost to run software is almost entirely the cost it consumes on the hardware and the network, which as we've just discussed is asymptotically approaching zero.

The cost to create software is almost entirely professional services. Because of the near zero cost of goods sold, software publishers have come up with many strategies for licensing to recoup their outlay. The ability of a software vendor to capture premium prices is based primarily on whether there is a perceived comparable competitor, and the switching cost to get to the competitor.

The cost to procure software that already exists depends on the licensing model, which is set by the owner / creator of the software.

The main licensing models that we will consider here are:

- One time (capitalized) cost – a firm can commission a software development firm to build software to their requirements. Once completed, the sponsor can do what they wish with it. Historically labor was expensed in the year incurred, but because of the costs and timeframes involved, most company now treat software development projects as capital expenses and put them on their balance sheet.

- Premise based / server based costs – if a software firm builds a software package for resale, their intent is to sell it to many firms and thereby recoup more than the cost they incurred. Their intent is to try to charge close to as much value as they are providing. In general, a large firm will be able to get more value out of a software system than a small firm. One way to extract more fees from a larger firm is using per user pricing (next bullet), but many firms build products for a given size firm and charge accordingly. QuickBooks has features and price points appropriate for very small firms and SAP has features and prices appropriate for the very large firms. These are usually adjusted for some proxy measures like number of servers, or number of cores.

- User or usage based – More and more software firms are pricing by some sort of meter: number of "named users" (people with unique logins), or "concurrent users" (number of users using the product at the same time), or transactions (number of interactions users have with the system). As software is moving to the cloud, more license models are becoming usage based.

- Maintenance and support – software has no "wear items" like the blades on a front-end loader or the teeth of a chain saw. It has no parts that degrade with use. And yet "maintenance" is a big part of software licensing, typically 15-20% annually of the original capital cost, which means that a system that survives 10 years has incurred twice as much maintenance costs as it did to create it. "Maintenance" is a gamble that the vendor will keep pace with changes in the software environment, and changes to the business and regulatory environment. You are betting that the vendor will have a version that supports the upgrade to the operating system that you will be installing. You are betting that they will supply required regulatory reports as laws change. "Support" (often bundled with Maintenance) is a retainer that provides for expert support on call in the event the system fails in production.

- Open source – more and more software is licensed under an open source license, which means that consumers of the software do not pay a license fee. The creation of the software consumed labor, but not conventionally. It came from developers who do this in their spare time, or from companies who employ developers and then contribute their output to an open source venue. The companies are often motivated either to get more developers working on the product (thereby improving its quality), or to gain notoriety for providing useful software.

Software, and therefore software licenses, exists at many layers in a firm's information infrastructure. There are operating systems licenses for servers as well as client devices. There is a vast number of software products at the infrastructure level that help processes work together better, including load balancing and integration software. There is software to manage databases, workflow messaging, and the like. Moreover, there is "application software" code that has been written to solve a specific business problem.

While many categories of software have become commoditized and have dropped dramatically in price, many other categories have moved in the opposite direction. The number of applications that a firm implements and manages has grown dramatically in the last few decades.

Software as a Service has already eclipsed new on-premise ERP implementations in some segments.[14]

As we will discuss later in this book, the attitude that business problems can be addressed by buying or building application systems, is at one level so obvious as to not merit mentioning, and at the same time is the primary root cause of the runaway dis-economy of most large enterprises information systems.

PROFESSIONAL SERVICES

This category covers all the technical specialists that are employed to build, maintain, or operate software systems. It includes a company's internal staff as well as consultants or outsourced contractors.

Gartner has estimated this to be a $900 billion industry, which employs 9 million professionals.[15]

The unit cost of professional services is the cost per hour to retain them—in other words, their salaries. The unit cost has remained relatively constant (adjusted for inflation) since the dawn of the computer age. Keep in mind this is at a time when most of the other cost components have dropped a million-fold or more.

---

[14] http://bit.ly/2kgZU7g.

[15] http://bit.ly/2C2rb5I.

What we would have hoped would have been that productivity would have climbed over this period of technological advancement.

Pundits often scoff at the transportation industry for not keeping pace. They say if the automotive industry had kept pace with the computer industry, a Rolls Royce would now cost 2 cents to purchase and get 200,000 miles to the gallon. This snide comment misses two important observations. There is a great disparity in the minimum size for each device. The original transistors were about the size of a grain of rice. Because there is no logical minimum size for a bit of information, transistors could keep shrinking—and they did.

Each reduction in size comes with a concomitant reduction in materials needed. An automobile must carry a passenger (typically two or four), and therefore its limit function is a contained space big enough for a family. The family will weigh 500+ pounds, so even a gossamer vehicle is going to weigh close to half a ton. If the transportation industry had kept pace, we could buy a Rolls Royce for pocket change, but it would fit on the head of a pin.

If we applied the analogy to the application software industry, we would say that we should be able to design and build a major application over a weekend.

To really humble ourselves, let's compare labor productivity to something more comparable: stevedoring (unloading ship cargo).

At the time of the birth of the computer industry, most cargo, and therefore most commerce, was carried by ship. An army of stevedores employed at each dock, loaded and unloaded the cargo from each vessel, and transferred it to the mode of its final mode of transportation (typically rail or truck).

In 1950 in New York, it took 1.9 person hours to handle a ton of cargo.[16]

By 2010, this had trickled down to 5 minutes a ton.[17] This was primarily achieved through the genius of containerization and cranes, as well as a bit of software to manage scheduling and sequencing. This is a 20-fold improvement in labor productivity.

One would think that laborers in the information processing industry might have achieved similar levels of productivity enhancement. We are the beneficiaries of over five decades of compounding improvements in all the factors that go into information systems. Hardware and networking costs have plummeted, there is an amazing selection of free or very cheap software to choose from, and we have been creating and applying improved methods for that entire time.

---

[16] The Box, Marc Levinson, 2nd Edition, Princeton University Press 2016, page 38.

[17] http://bit.ly/2AJ8wLR. p 71.

Researchers claim, correctly, that information system professional's productivity is hard to measure. This is true, but let's look at some macro statistics:

- Labor Unit Costs have been mostly flat, except for the trend toward offshoring, which has had a moderating effect

- Adjusted for inflation, professional salaries have been relatively flat for the last 50 years[18]

- Overall number of hours spent by information processing professionals has grown considerably over the last five decades

Are we processing that much more information? Yes, we have big data, so at one level we are running a lot more information through our pipes. But for many companies, the core number of transactions has not grown so rapidly. If you are a manufacturing company, you could easily be building the same number of widgets. You may capture more data points along the way, but this is all in service of doing a better job of building those widgets.

Hardware, networking, software licensing, and professional services are the four fundamental factors of production in software implementation. How they interact and how they have changed over time has

---

[18] http://bit.ly/2kTyzXB.

shaped the forces that are driving the consumption of these resources.

HOW INFORMATION SYSTEM COSTS REALLY BEHAVE

Now that we have a shared understanding of how the component costs have changed over the last several decades, let's explore the more complex contributors to the runaway and widespread waste.

While the cost to deploy and host a system has dropped dramatically in the last several decades, the cost to implement and run a major application has gone up rather than down. We owe it to ourselves to find out why.

So where is all that money going, and why?

Our contention is that the real cost drivers are the following, which have received not nearly enough attention:

- Complexity
- Dependency
- Integration
- People change management
- Cost of application functionality change

COMPLEXITY

A complex system is one made of many interrelated parts. The level of complexity is driven by the number of parts and especially by the nature of their interrelationships. There are many formal ways to measure the complexity of computer programs, such as the McCabe Cyclomatic Complexity measure or Halstead metrics. The McCabe Cyclomatic Complexity examines the number of potential paths through a particular piece of code. Halstead metrics focus on the cognitive load on attempting to understand the software. The Halstead metrics count things like the vocabulary size and the number of operators and operands.

While these can gauge the complexity of a program, the key issue is not the complexity of individual programs but the complexity of having and relying on literally, thousands of individual programs, many of which interact with each other, in hard to predict ways.

DEPENDENCY

One aspect of complexity that amplifies the problem is dependency. Some component B is dependent on a component A if any change to A affects B.

The following diagram contains a greatly abridged portion of a dependency analysis we did for a client. At the top of the diagram are applications, followed by databases, languages, infrastructure, operating systems, Application Programming Interfaces (APIs), and hardware—any of which might form the basis for dependency.

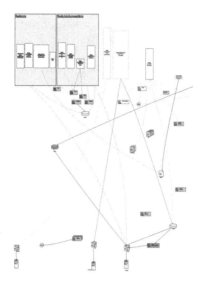

For instance, if a program calls a subroutine, and someone changes that subroutine, there is a very good chance that the calling program will be adversely impacted.

A system with 1 million independent components is not unthinkably complex; it is just a collection of parts that do not interact. The number of bottles in the following picture does not make the system complex.

A system with 1000 components that are mutually and intimately interdependent can be impossibly complex.

The issue with many enterprise systems is that the stewards of the system often are unaware of the nature of the dependencies. When you are unaware of the dependencies, the only conservative options are to make no changes, or to examine and test every possibly affected component.

The obvious dependencies between programs are rarely to blame for making dependency so pernicious in enterprise systems. There are dependencies that cross levels. For instance, there are dependencies between application software and infrastructure software. There are dependencies between code and metadata, and between metadata and data.

As we will explore later in this book, these dependencies tend to keep legacy systems locked in.

INTEGRATION

Integration is the act of getting subsystems that were independently developed to interoperate. It is generally viewed as a high value-added activity. This is mainly because we haven't recognized that it was the independent development of things that should have been integrated, that eventually leads to the need for integration.

The cost of integrations should be viewed in the same way the manufacturing industry sees rework. That is, as waste. The rework itself isn't waste, always better to fix something before you ship it, but the rework is an indicator of the extent of the waste in the manufacturing process.

We should view the entire systems integration industry as an indication of the waste that we have engineered into our application implementation practices.

PEOPLE CHANGE MANAGEMENT

Large systems projects have large "change management" programs. This is the activity of getting a lot of people to simultaneously change the way they work in order to implement a new system, or often to implement an improved workflow.

In large systems projects this can consume as much as a third of the project budget. The surface reason for why it costs so much is that the software package already exists, and can be acquired for a low price. Changing the software is very expensive, so the preferred approach is to change the organization to accommodate the software. Generally, executives claim that this is adopting "best practices" but often that is just an excuse.

It is hard to change people's processes because we so rarely understand them. In a mature organization, most of the workforce has learned their function from the systems they use. They have learned the vocabulary from the terms presented in the user interface. They have adapted their workflow to accommodate that which is imposed by the system. They have even built workarounds to compensate for the shortcomings of the system.

Much of this is tacit. People have internalized this and it is how they do their job. Even small changes to workflow or terminology are difficult to master. Wholesale changes are especially hard.

But it needn't be this way. This is a product of the new system being both inflexible and arbitrary. The inflexibility will be discussed in the next section. Because the system was designed and built for another context and use, it becomes arbitrary. It is possible that the current system is a good match but often it is not.

COST OF APPLICATION FUNCTIONALITY CHANGE

The single most important metric, and one that virtually no one measures, is the cost of making a change to an application system.

People estimate change projects, but they generally do this on a project-by-project basis. As such, they are unable to compare the cost of a change in one system to the cost in another. In addition, they have no way of knowing where they stand with their competitors.

The reasons for not tracking this metric are many, but I suspect the two biggest contributors are:

- There is no common denominator between changes

- There is no linear relationship between the change and the cost

No common denominator between changes

Not all changes are equal in complexity. Typically, the cost of changing the layout of existing fields on a screen or a form is far less than the cost of adding fields to a screen or a form. Moreover, adding fields to a screen or a form is typically far easier than adding columns to a database, which in turn is easier than a change to the structure of the database.

The other reason for reluctance is that most change requests are bundles of individual changes. However, this excuse shouldn't be enough to avoid doing what is required. By retreating from the task of predicting and measuring the cost of change, a firm is unlikely to see where its real problems lie, and this blinds them to the real source of their legacy diseconomies.

We believe there are a small set of types of changes. A change request could easily be decomposed into a certain number of each type.

No linear relationship between the change and the cost

The other reason people don't measure cost of change is that they believe it will be futile. They believe there isn't a relationship between the change and the effort. They believe this because their experience tells them this is so.

But what almost everyone has not factored in, and is the difference that makes this whole problem tractable, is that the cost of a change is not proportional to the complexity of the change. The cost of change is proportional to the complexity of the thing being changed.

Adding a field to a recently developed agile system is fairly easy. Adding a field to an ERP system could be an entire career. The biggest multiplier effect comes when a change affects not just a complex system, but other dependent components and systems.

We worked with a Workers Compensation Insurance Company. An injured worker sued, and won, a case that established that the insurance company had to pay an injured worker not just for their lost wages, but also some percent of the health insurance premium that was being picked up by their employer while they were working. This court case established the new precedent and the company was obligated to comply, not just for the immediate case but for all other cases.

On the surface, this was a reasonably small change to make to their systems. They would need some screens to ask the injured worker how much medical insurance they were receiving through their work. They would need a few more screens to verify this information with the employer. They would also need an algorithm to determine how much of this would be added to the claimant's benefits.

Rather than the simple set of changes I just described, the actual change cost over a million dollars and took the better part of a year to implement. Were these people incompetent? No, anything but. But the systems environment was far more complex than would have been imagined. In the first place, there wasn't one system. There were systems to manage self-insured companies. There was the standard Workers Compensation claims system. There was a pension-based claims system. There were interfaces between these systems and dozens of auxiliary systems, many of which were affected. The data warehouse was affected, as were the ETL (Extract, Transform, and Load) processes that fed the data warehouse.

This drove home the idea that the cost of change is not driven by the complexity of the *change*, but the complexity of *the thing being changed*.

It is our contention that a firm that tracked their changes this way would rapidly become wise. Their wisdom would be in understanding the characteristics of their existing systems that lead to high cost of change. Moreover, once they knew this, they would move with much more confidence toward systematically reducing their legacy burden.

SUMMARY

In any other industry, reducing the cost of your key inputs by a million fold would reduce the cost of the end product significantly. That the cost of implementing enterprise application keeps going up should give us pause and make us wonder whether we are subtly sabotaging ourselves.

We've been struck by this contradiction for two decades. Over that time we have examined several hundred projects, some unmitigated disasters, some marginally successful. We've done root cause analysis. We have been looking for what is behind this situation. Most of the bromides that have been floated to fix these problems (better project management, better methodologies, better tools, better technologies) are at best very tangential, and at worse red herrings. We will examine many of these in Chapter 4, but we will put forward our contention for the primary drivers for the current state of the art: the application-centric mindset coupled with attraction to unnecessary complexity.

CHAPTER 3
The application-centric
mindset

There is a mindset referred to as "the IT application-centric mindset" which has led the industry to its current intractable place. This mindset promotes the proliferation of overlapping solutions and at the same time making each solution far more complex than needed. Let's examine what the application mindset looks like, and where it comes from. A typical business application is often depicted like this:

User Interface   Business Logic   Data

This is called the "three tier architecture." The belief is that an application can be "layered" with each layer largely independent. This prevalent approach is called "application-centric."

This approach starts off with someone wanting an application built or implemented. The requirements of the application dictate the scope of the data in the database which determines what will be in the logic layer which further determines what is presented in the user interface.

The application-centric approach leads to three main problems:

- Instead of separation of concerns we have harmful dependency

- The stack fosters runaway redundancy

- We have a breeding ground for unnecessary complexity

Let's look at how this happens.

DEPENDENCY

Firstly, far from being independent, the three layers mostly act as a single monolith. Imagine a very simple one-form application containing a database with one table and four columns, a user interface with one form and four fields, and logic that mediates the two.

If you wish to have another field on your form, you first must change all three levels: add the new field to the database, display the field on the user interface, and perhaps add logic to validate data for this new field.

In the best architectures, the following are managed in the business logic layer:

- **Validation.** For example, make sure entered data matches its field types.

- **Security.** For example, make sure the staff can't see salary data.

- **Identity management.** For example, make sure if we've encountered this patient before we use the same patient id.

- **Business logic.** For example, make sure the "from date" on a task is before the "to date."

- **Meaning.** For example, if there is a "CR" in the account type field then the values in the amount field should be multiplied by -1.

As we'll mention in a bit, it is bad enough that this is managed in the business layer; it is generally worse if this logic is managed only in the user interface client layer.

What this ends up doing is preventing the possibility of anyone accessing the data directly, because to do so would obviate the security, identity management, validation, business logic, and meaning. Almost all enterprise applications prevent direct access to their databases, and instead, if access is granted at all, it is through APIs.

The intention of this layering was to reduce dependency. Yet in almost all cases, there is greater dependency. The database is completely dependent on the middle layer, in that there is so much essential logic in there that it would be imprudent to allow access to the database without going through the middle layer. The middle layer is in turn dependent on the database, as any change to the database schema and the middle layer is broken. The top layer is dependent on the middle layer, as it is the only way to get to the data.

In most architectures, the middle layer is dependent on the user interface layer, in that the fields on the forms are reflected in, and often created by logic in the middle layer. If the form were to change, then the middle layer would not work.

The data layer is dependent on the user interface layer. In general, if the business requirements dictate that a new field is needed on a form, the database must change to accommodate it.

Every piece of this architecture is dependent on every other piece.

REDUNDANCY

When businesses were small and applications were small and few in number, the application-centric architecture was still workable. And it was the best we had.

However, as application projects grew in size and cost, there was a legitimate backlash and a desire to fund less ambitious projects.

A smaller application with its own small database, small logic, and small user interface, could be scoped, managed, and executed in a predictable amount of time.

If all these small applications were completely independent, this wouldn't create a problem. But that isn't the case at all. Virtually all parts of an enterprise are deeply connected. Attempts to partition off small bits end up partitioning off highly redundant bits.

We had a client that managed workplace safety for the State of Washington, which included permits and licenses. Scoping an elevator permit receivables system as a separate project is possible. There is a cost, though. Redundantly implementing the idea of a customer or a landlord (the owner of the elevator) leads to redundancy of the inspectors (who no doubt are also employees of the agency and therefore show up in other systems), as well as redundancy of cash application (because the landlord may also be an employer and therefore may owe money for other reasons).

This would merely be bad if all these implementations used exactly the same data structures, validation, business logic, security, identity management, and semantics from one application to another. However, it's much worse.

In most enterprises, half or more of these applications are packaged software, so there is no hope that they have similar data structures, validation, business logic, security, identity management, or semantics.

Further, across different applications, whether they are packages or not, each project seems to have perverse ways of development at different layers of abstraction. Some designer decides the design will be "table driven" or "parametric" or "configurable"; this essentially means that the problem was solved at a different level of abstraction. Where one system might have two different columns for single-family mortgage value and multiple family mortgage value, another system might have one field for amount and another one next to it that says "mortgage type." And yet another one might have a field called "field type" which points to a table which points to another table that says this is a mortgage type, and then points to yet another table to find out what type it is.

The net of all this is a three-layer architecture (user-interface, logic, and data) with deep interdependencies, and as we'll see in the next section, high degree of complexity. This complexity encourages the creation of large numbers of applications, which unfortunately are highly overlapped.

However, what makes the problem intractable is the complexity of these systems.

COMPLEXITY

What is strange is how complex most of these application systems are. Complexity is multiplying the sheer numbers of things by the number and type of interrelationships between those things.

A spreadsheet with 10,000 people's names on it is perhaps a bit more complex than one with 1,000 names on it. However, changing a name in the list has no effect on any other name in the list. A spreadsheet with 1,000 cells containing formulas that refer to each other is much more complex because changing either the value or the formula in a cell may have all sorts of unpredictable effects on the rest of the spreadsheet.

When a manufacturer produces more and more of the same item, the unit costs go down; this is referred to as "economies of scale." Each doubling of production tends to deliver a constant reduction in unit price. The constant is different depending on the type of manufacturing. For instance, you should expect that the millionth soap dispenser will cost about 5% less than the 500,000th one, which in turn was 5% less expensive than the 250,000[th] one. As you make more you find ways to economize.

It is very seductive to believe that if we could get a software factory cranking out code that the unit cost would go down.

However, in reality, just the opposite happens. The more code you have, the more each incremental unit costs you.

This is because of the complexity difference. The 1,000,001[st] soap dispenser cares little about the other 1 million. The 1,000,001[st] line of code in a project must fit in with, and not violate the other 1 million–a task that just grows harder as the numbers get bigger.

There is complexity at all three levels because each layer is dependent on each other layer.

In addition, many humans and most (but not all) of the developers I have met in my career like complexity. More accurately, they like *just the right amount* of complexity.

Someone using a spreadsheet to solve a problem often grafts new aspects of the problem onto an existing structure. Some add in nicely, and some challenge what has already been done. Inevitably, additions make the sum more complex.

The designer is gradually getting familiar with the complex edifice he or she has built. They have internalized a certain part of the complexity. Because they have, each increment is not too much of a burden.

However, someone coming to it anew will find the sum total of complexity intimidating. I've become convinced that most designers and developers like this. It gives them something between a sense of pride and a sense of superiority to have mastered this thing that others cannot fathom. It provides job security. Therefore, at the micro level there is little incentive to simplify.

Some understand the trap that this is. At one level, even the master of a complex system, if they are away from it for months will return and be at least partially as puzzled as the novice. In addition, some recognize that the power of exclusive knowledge is also a trap; they may be prevented from moving on because of their irreplaceable skill.

Fortunately, there are those few who find simplicity to be its own reward. When an agile programmer "refactors" their code, they are noting that the accretion of many changes has created some unnecessary complication; a rearrangement of the code can create a new, simpler, and better solution. For agile practitioners this is almost a spiritual quest.

> *Software entities are more complex for their size than perhaps any other human construct, because no two parts are alike.*
>
> Fredrick Brooks[19]

---

[19] http://bit.ly/209mWyd.

The Fredrick Brooks quote above is from a seminal article he wrote called "No Silver Bullet: Essence and Accident in Software Engineering." In that article he puts forward the astute observation that there are two types of complexity in software systems: the essential (which is the complexity inherent in the problem to be solved) and the accidental (which is the complexity introduced in the approaches and tools used in the solution).

Fredrick says unless accidental complexity is more than $9/10^{th}$ of the complexity in a system, then reducing it to 0 will not result in an order of magnitude improvement. He believed that accidental complexity could not be more that 90% of the complexity of a solution. This might have been true in the 1960's when he was honing his craft. My observation is that runaway complexity is the key issue for our industry. It is the equivalent of the quality revolution for the manufacturing industry.

Our observation is that individual systems usually have 10 times as much accidental complexity as essential and that systems of systems (the vast interrelated set of applications that run most enterprises) have ratios that are 100 to 1000 times as much accidental complexity as essential. Eliminating accidental complexity is the most important thing most firms can do.

THE HUMAN MIND

There are limitations to the amount of complexity the human mind can deal with, as George Miller pointed out in the famous article "The Magical Number Seven, plus or minus two":

> *"The average human's short term memory can handle seven things at a time. We can keep a grocery list of seven items in our mind, we remember seven-digit numbers, etc. The plus or minus two refers to both differences between individuals and differences in circumstances."*[20]

We augment our limited short-term memory with all sorts of strategies. We use repetition, chunking, rhyming, anchoring, and many other techniques to allow us to retrain and track far more than this. While we have vocabularies of tens of thousands of words, we typically have only a handful of them in our short-term memory at any point in time.

One of the most powerful ways to augment our limited attention spans is through writing, and especially drawing. Writing captures a great deal of information, but we still end up processing sequentially when we read it.

LEVELING

Jorge Luis Borges inserted a reference to a short fictitious story about a society of mapmakers who created a map so precise that it was as large as the

---

[20] Miller, G. A. (1956). "The magical number seven, plus or minus two: Some limits on our capacity for processing information". Psychological Review. 63 (2): 81–97. doi:10.1037/h0043158. PMID 13310704.

empire it was attempting to describe.[21] Ultimately, the populace revolted and rejected the maps as being more cumbersome than useful.

A map is useful to the extent that it reduces complexity while retaining important aspects of the thing it is describing. Many useful maps of the same territory may highlight different aspects while ignoring others. A subway map can emphasize sequence and interconnectedness while relaxing geospatial precision.

Mapmakers have discovered this. A road map typically unfolds to the three by four-foot size. Most road maps have far more than 200 items on them, but it is rare that you take in anything near that in a one-minute viewing. You may peruse a road map of Manhattan for a minute and take in central park, the boroughs, the bodies of water, and several dozen streets, neighborhoods, and key buildings that you are looking for.

In the old days if you wanted to drive across the country you might have one (three by four foot) map of the country you are in. (Did it ever seem odd that every country regardless of its size has a map that is three by four feet in dimension?) Let's say you were driving across the United States. You would have one map to plan your overall route, and then you might well have another

---

[21] J. L. Borges, *A Universal History of Infamy* (translated by Norman Thomas de Giovanni), Penguin Books, London, 1975. ISBN 0-14-003959-7.

three by four-foot map for any cities or parks you wanted to explore in more detail. There are details in the city maps that aren't in the country maps.

This may sound a bit anachronistic in an age of interactive maps on your smart phone. But consider this in the context of Nicholas Carr's observations in "Is Google Making Us Stupid?"[22] I would contend that Google Maps is making us geospatially stupid. When we look at the map on our smart phone (if we look at it at all), we are looking at a handful of attributes. We do not know where we are contextually (unless we zoom out at which point we lose a lot of detail).[23]

And so it is with models.

A model with more than a few hundred concepts needs to be "leveled." If your ERP system has 20,000 tables and nearly a million attributes, it is impossible to draw a map of the system at any level of resolution.

Leveling is essentially delegating to another mind. In delegating, you have greatly reduced the coordination and integration that would be possible if you did not delegate.

---

[22] http://theatln.tc/2lw3T3f.

[23] This was independently verified recently in a conversation with Patrick Conway the head of Knowledge Management for the US Army Tradocs, who told me that only 20% of incoming army inductees could read a map (an important skill for combatants in foreign countries).

Let's say it is your job to understand a complex system such as an ERP system. If you are lucky, you can find or create a map that tells you how the 50 main subsystems fit together. You delegate to someone one of those boxes (let's say the Classification Engine, as I met someone who was a worldwide expert in the SAP classification engine).

The classification engine itself is a complex system, with 200 plus interacting components.

APPLICATION CENTRICITY AND COMPLEXITY MATH

Here is how this comes together. The total complexity of your application scape is:

(Number of applications) * Schema * Code = Complexity

Study after study has shown that the average number of errors in a software system (which gives you the number of changes that need to be made) and the cost of making them go up with the size of the code base. At the first level of approximation, the number of lines of code is a very good proxy for complexity and cost.

What this formula tells us, is if we could reduce the value of any one of the factors contributing to code and therefore cost and complexity, we would reduce the overall cost and complexity by a proportional amount. That is, if we cut the number of supported applications in half (and kept the other two factors constant), our overall cost of system support would drop by half. Because these three factors are products of each other, if you can reduce two or three of them simultaneously the total comes down even faster. Let's look at this a bit closer:

- **Number of applications**. This refers only to applications that your firm is actively managing – so not your copies of Microsoft Word.

- **Schema**. This is the number of schema distinctions (typically tables and columns) that must be coded to. There are a few situations where increasing the schema size does not increase the amount of code needed in the application, so we want to exclude those cases.

- **Code per schema**. In any given environment, you can roughly predict the number of lines of code in the application based on the complexity of the schema. This is a rough constant based on the programming language and system environment.

For many applications, it is easier to derive the third term from the first two and the total.

I have this fascination with QuickBooks. I've used it for years. I've often wondered how complex it is, and how complex it needs to be. I did a bit of research and found that QuickBooks is one application (they actually have one code base for a large number of variations in the product, which is cool); the schema consists of approximately 150 tables and 7,500 attributes, so it has 7,650 schema concepts that must be coded to. Further, I found out that the code base is 10 million lines of code. The third factor, code per schema, then, is 1,300 lines of code per schema concept.

Once you get past one application the second and third factor are averages. Identify the average schema complexity and the average number of lines of code per schema. Let's look at each in turn:

- **Drop the number of applications**. This is where many people are focused now: application rationalization. If you find you have many applications performing the same function, combine them to reduce overall costs.

- **Schema per app**. Until you change the way you design apps this is not going to improve. RESTful APIs improve this somewhat, especially if the RESTful endpoint treats each request as a generalized query.

- **Code per schema**. This has the potential to go to close to zero. The "Low code / no code" movement and "Model Driven Development" teach us that a well-architected system needs to introduce very little new code, even when the schema doubles in size.

If you drop any one of the factors in half, the total drops in half. If you drop two of them in half the total drops by

75% and if you drop all three in half the total drops by 83%.

Reducing the complexity of any of these by half isn't even hard, given where they started. If you drop the complexity of any of these by an order of magnitude, the total goes down by 90%. Two dropped by an order of magnitude and the result is a reduction of two orders of magnitude (99%) reduction, and if you reduce all three by an order of magnitude, the total goes down by three orders of magnitude (by 99.9%).

I know how unbelievable this sounds. I've been in business for a long time, and I know that incredible claims are met with disbelief, but at some point, some people are going to look at the economics and be chagrinned by what they have tolerated. Dropping any one of these by an order of magnitude shouldn't even cause you to break a sweat. All three is a bit of a stretch, but doesn't violate any laws of physics or indeed any best practices.

SUMMARY

Are the people who charge $1 billion for a $1 million system crooks, idiots, or heroes?

If you believe that these simple systems are complex and should cost $1 billion, then a firm that can complete it for $1 billion is a hero. I find no evidence that these projects are even within two orders of magnitude of their "should cost" numbers.

If you agree with my observations, you are left with this question: Are these people crooks or idiots? Do they know these are million dollar systems but they have created a scheme to convince people that they cost and are therefore worth 1,000 times that? In other words are these the DeBeers of the software implementation business (the DeBeers know that diamonds are fairly common, but have managed for over 100 years to control the supply and pump up the demand, such that jewelry grade diamonds command at least 10 times their free market value).

I have worked for some of these companies. I have partnered with others; I have observed them at close quarters on many projects we have worked on.

I'm going to give them the benefit of the doubt. I think they are idiots. That is, I think they sincerely believe that they are executing these projects at the limit of their capability and they believe they are "this hard." I have not worked with the so-called "beltway bandits" who know that these projects should / could be a tiny fraction of what they are, but they are more than happy to compete for projects that have been inflated to 100 times their economic necessity.

I am completely convinced that the two pillars of runaway waste are the application-centric mindset and the complexity imperative.

CHAPTER 4
Why what we've tried
before hasn't helped

It is not the case that people don't realize that
application implementation is difficult and expensive.
It's not like there haven't been attempts in the past to
address this. As we'll see though, each attempt either has
a fatal flaw at its core, or it is only one part of a holistic
solution.

The main approaches tried in the past have been:

- Relational databases
- ERP systems
- Enterprise data modeling
- Service-oriented architecture and APIs
- Agile
- Data warehouses and business intelligence

- Outsourcing and offshoring
- Cloud
- Software as a Service (SaaS)
- Data lakes
- Machine learning and artificial intelligence

RELATIONAL DATABASES

Relational databases were such a breakthrough advantage over their predecessors (mostly hierarchical and CODASYL databases) that it is sometimes hard to imagine they are not the final answer. Hierarchical databases like IBM's IMS and HP's IME stored information in predefined trees. The trees were domain specific such as orders to order lines, or ledgers to sub ledgers. CODASYL databases stored everything in linked lists, which make it rapid to traverse a persisted array. It probably wasn't the technology itself that doomed these databases; it was more likely the reaction to their proprietary interfaces. Once you committed to one of these platforms, all the code was written to that API (Application Programming Interface) and there was no possibility of porting it to another vendor, let alone another style of database.

Relational came along with two breakthrough ideas: a standard, declarative interface (SQL) and the flexibility of table structures. For years, relational suffered a performance disadvantage to the established and highly tuned hierarchical and CODASYL databases. Over time, the advantages of the declarative interface won out.

With a declarative interface, you state what you want, without procedurally describing how the system will get this information. In the short term, being able to describe which data set to access first or which linked list to use to traverse, gave developers of older systems more tricks to use to goose performance. Ultimately, the relational database vendors were able to gather statistics about the distribution of keys in tables, and were able to change their query plan on the fly, which ultimately resulted in faster query times and more flexibility. In addition, of course, the million-fold reduction in hardware costs meant that professional services hard coding solutions to wring a bit more performance out of the system were less and less economical.

So, why do we call this an approach that hasn't worked? To be fair we should say that it has overshot it effectiveness. While it was a great choice for most of the 1990's and even into the 2000's, it is now becoming part of the problem.

The problems are:

- Non-portability
- Inability to interoperate
- Human in the loop
- Promotion of complexity
- Difficulty in scaling

NON-PORTABILITY

One of the big selling points for relational databases was that they could be accessed with a single standard access language, SQL. There is still an "ANSI SQL Standard." However, this is just a starting point for all vendor-specific implementations of relational databases.

I worked on an early relational project using DEC's (Digital Equipment Corporation) RDB. One of the great and appreciated things about the user manual for this database was that it was written in two colors. The black text described how the ANSI SQL features worked and the red text explained how the DEC supplied features worked.

Perhaps they thought this was a way to demonstrate how much fuller featured their product was than one that only supported the standard. Or maybe they did this for the developers who were keen to stick with the standards-only feature.

I referred to this manual as "the new testament," because there was more red text than black.

Other vendors did the same thing and extended the standard. Developers seem all too eager to use a feature that solves a problem rather than spend any time worrying whether the feature is nonstandard.

At this point, the result was that it was prohibitively expensive to migrate an application from one SQL database to another. To convert an enterprise application system from say Oracle to Microsoft SQL or IBM's DB2 (or vice versa) would typically be a multi-million dollar, multi-year project, which most companies rightfully try to avoid.

INABILITY TO INTEROPERATE

Related to and exacerbated by the previous, is the difficulty in interoperating between databases. A SQL DBMS (Database Management System) is the engine that interprets the SQL requests. These DBMSs have been very tuned for rapid access to the database they are attached to.

Trying to query across two databases is very difficult. Trying to join two databases from different vendors is even more so. There has been little effort, and few tools for federating queries across databases.

This has further encouraged the "siloing" of data. What you will typically see in most enterprises is a one-to-one mapping of applications to databases. There is a Payroll Database to support the Payroll application and an HR Database to support the HR application. Instead of federating to another database to augment your application with shared data, the preferred method is to write a batch and / or asynchronous program that will load copies of the other data into the application database where the joining and performance can be locally managed.

This is what is contributing to the proliferation of databases, and the consumption of the IT budget in writing and maintaining interfaces.

As we will describe in the companion book, a number of more modern technologies and approaches will address these problems.

HUMAN IN THE LOOP

The flexibility of relational comes at a cost. All data is stored in tables. For instance in this table we have secret agents:

agent		
Id	Last Name	Full Name
006	Renton	Andy Renton
007	Bond	James Bond

The tables all have a fixed number of columns, and each column has a name. The columns of a table are related to the row, and tables can be "related" to each other, hence the name "relational."

However, the consumer of the data must pre-specify how that "relation" is to be made.

For instance, if we want to assign gadgets to secret agents, we do that by putting the agent's ID in the "AssnTo" column of the gadget table:

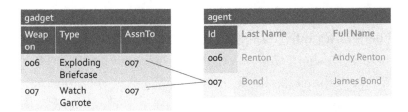

Note that while "007" refers to Bond in the id of the Agent table and the AssnTo of the Gadget table, the "007" in the Weapon column does not refer to Bond.

If we want to find out the name of each agent assigned to each gadget, we write a query that "joins" these tables:

```
SELECT Gadget.Type Agent.FullName
FROM Gadget, Agent
WHERE Gadget.AssnTo = Agent.Id
```

This hand crafting of joins at query authoring time is no longer necessary in many post relational system, but persists because it is necessary in the relational world.

This may not sound too bad when we are working through pedagogical examples with a handful of tables, but as we describe in the next section, that is not what we have implemented in relational systems.

PROMOTION OF COMPLEXITY

The relational database has promoted complexity at two levels: the data design and application code.

Data design complexity

There is no inheritance mechanism in relational. If you have a concept that is similar to another concept, but differs perhaps in that it needs a few extra columns, you have two choices: extend the existing table or create a new one. Since extending the existing table may mean rewriting code, we often create a new table to handle the extra columns.

The net effect of making many small changes such as this over many years is profound. Most relational databases that we have examined are orders of magnitude more complex than they need to be. That is, the total number of tables and columns are 10-100 times greater than necessary if the system was implemented efficiently in a modern environment.

As mentioned earlier, in large application systems, there are often thousands of tables and tens of thousands of columns. This represents a large hurdle for someone attempting to use or maintain the system.

By the way, there is also a perverse incentive for keeping the complexity. If it takes years to master the data model for an application, anyone who has mastered it has job security. If it was developed in-house, the company becomes dependent on these key resources. If this is a package, the knowledgeable consultant has an attractive career.

There are several forces pushing relational databases to even higher levels of complexity. As these systems become more complex, they spawn a second order complexity effect: more and more complex code.

Application code complexity

Relational systems sprung up around the same time as structured programming. Structured programming was a discipline that strongly suggested that the structure of an application program should mirror the structure of the database that it was accessing. The tools and programs that people use to write application code that accesses relational databases tend to mirror the data structures.

There is a belief that the application code that accesses the relational database contains a great deal of business logic or algorithms. It does not. If you look long and hard at application code that accesses relational databases, you will find that 90% or more of the code is very repetitive and simplistic. There is some logic that says things like "if the value in the 'into-go-down-marker' is '1' then subtract the balance from the on-hand value." This may pass for business logic, but it is working around bad design.

The sum total of profligate tables added to the fact that every new table virtually guarantees thousands of additional lines of trivial application code that must be written, tested, and eventually maintained, results in even medium-sized applications ending up with millions of lines of code.

DIFFICULTY IN SCALING

There are two scale issues with relational: the number of rows to be processed and the number of tables that must be joined.

The two issues compound each other. In small volume systems, you can join dozens of tables and still get reasonable performance. Furthermore, if you are not joining many tables you can access a billion-row table and still get reasonable performance.

The problem lies in between. Queries with millions of rows and dozens of table joins can be especially hard to tune. This is the juncture that "big data" was introduced to solve.

ERP SYSTEMS

ERP (Enterprise Resource Planning) was meant to be the system that would solve all of our integration problems. To understand ERP, we need to go back a bit and trace its roots.

In the early days of business systems, we had functional point solutions. A company typically had separate Accounts Receivable and Accounts Payable systems, separate Purchasing and Inventory Control Systems, etc. Occasionally these would be from the same vendor, and sometimes they would talk to each other.

Manufacturing companies had problems that are more complex and needed to integrate more point solutions. At one point, "MRP" (Manufacturing Resource Planning) systems were created and sold that organized many of the subsidiary systems around the manufacturing companies "Bill of Materials" (the hierarchical structure of how parts went into sub-assemblies, which in turn went into bigger sub-assemblies and up the line until complex products could be designed and built). These integrated systems subsumed applications like inventory control and shop floor control as tight integration was needed to make them work.

As usual with a breakthrough idea that works, many knockoffs appeared in the industry. These knockoffs weren't integrated well and didn't provide the benefits that the first generation had. In a marvelous bit of rebranding, the industry decided that the old wine in new bottles would be called MRP II (to distinguish it from the MRP systems that were losing favor).

MRP II became a big deal for manufacturers. However, someone noticed that these MRP II systems still had to be integrated with Finance, HR, and a few other systems. The thought occurred: rather than incur the integration costs, why not start with a system that is already integrated?

It was recognized in the 1980's that integration between applications was a problem, and that one potential solution was to have a single integrated database. If you could build all your applications on a single database, there would be no need for integration.

Thus was born ERP (Enterprise Resource Planning). SAP from Germany lead the way, and still dominates this category, with competition primarily from Oracle at the high end. There are many mid-market ERP vendors out there.

As one watches the evolution of the ERP market, a few fascinating trends emerge. First, the systems became more and more complex. Each generation added features and tables to cover more and more possibilities "out of the box." The data schemas have become immense. A typical SAP installation now has 90,000 tables and 1,000,000 columns.[24]

The other fascinating thing is how the scope of an ERP project continues to shrink even as the cost of the project increases. It used to be that an ERP system was firm-wide, and covered most of the functions touched by the supply chain and the manufacturing process and the order to cash cycles.

Nowadays most ERP implementations are single function. We often see an HR implementation touted as an ERP implementation, or a Finance project as an ERP implementation. Indeed, more and more ERP implementations are now with firms that don't

---

[24] Private conversation with representatives from Silwood Technology a firm that specializes in reversing engineering ERP implementations.

manufacture anything. The current growth market for ERP systems is government agencies, which they are ill-suited to address.

The amazing thing is that very few large firms have managed to get even all of their manufacturing-related functionality onto a single integrated database. We rarely see more than about 20-30% of the core functionality managed by the ERP system. What this means is the original benefit (of avoiding integration costs by having everything on the single database) have not been achieved and the firm must still invest a great deal in integration. The sad thing is that, having chased the ERP dream, they are now saddled with an environment that is very hard to integrate because of its internal complexity.

As the costs and risks of implementing integrated systems rose, and the timetables dragged on, business users found themselves compelled to implement smaller, satellite programs to implement the functionality they needed. Rather than add Order Returns functionality to the ERP system, it seemed easier to build (or buy) a system that did returns. Rather than add Operating Rooms scheduling to the Electronic Medical Record, it was easier to buy one.

The result is the worst of all possible worlds: the firm adopts a dis-economic platform that might eliminate the cost of integration with a host of other applications, spawned by the very dis-economy it was trying to avoid.

The complexity of this integrated "system of systems" leads to a core that is the most expensive possible system to implement, and a growing number of satellite systems that also require integration.

To prove that truth is stranger than fiction, most very large firms have dozens of ERP systems, most of which don't talk to each other, let alone to non-ERP systems. One very large company we know of, partly due to acquisitions, ended up with 88 ERP systems, five of which were integrated with each other.

What started life as a reasonable expectation (with the sentiment of "let's not re-invent the wheel") became the excuse to launch projects that were vastly more expensive and riskier than the very thing they were being held up against (i.e. custom development).

ENTERPRISE DATA MODELING

Recognizing that they weren't going to get all their functionality onto one database, in the 1990's many large firms embraced the idea that if they just had a shared data model, it would reduce their integration costs and guide future application development. Both these observations were true, but universally failed to pan out.

One reason they didn't pan out, was that they were embarking on this quest just as business users were doubling down on package applications (which needless to say, did not conform to the enterprise data model).

Another reason this didn't solve the problem was that the timeframes stretched too far, exceeding any reasonable planning horizons. It was not uncommon for an enterprise data modeling project to take two to three years, and was very common that it would get cancelled before it was completed.

The final reason it didn't solve the problems was the belief that the enterprise data model needed to be three cross referenced models (a "conceptual model" using end user terminology, a "logical model" which mapped the conceptual model onto a normalized data structure, and a "physical model" which included considerations needed for performance and scale). The conceptual model could not be implemented directly and was seen as academic. The logical model also couldn't be implemented directly, and in any case, would only be implemented in custom applications. All changes had to be introduced in and cross-referenced to all three models.

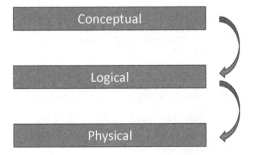

The few firms that completed enterprise data models had models of such complexity (30,000 entities for the IRS) that the exercise generally doomed the implementation.

SERVICE-ORIENTED ARCHITECTURE AND APIS

Service-Oriented Architecture (SOA) and the Enterprise Service Bus (ESB) evolved as some enlightened firms figured out that they were stuck with lots of "siloed" systems, and their best hope was organizing a way for them to communicate, rather than allow things to devolve into a series of ad hoc point-to-point interfaces.

The early implementers of SOA mostly "rolled their own" as there were no products to buy. They built their solutions very intentionally to replace point-to-point interfaces with shared messaging. There were some early and impressive successes.

Software vendors took note, and built packaged SOA or ESB products. ESB (Enterprise Service Bus) was a platform that could be purchased to implement an SOA.[25] Firms bought these solutions believing that the package was the solution. Alas, the package is just the possibility of a solution. Generally, the solution involves a lot of discipline, and buying a package is no substitute for discipline.

Most companies that bought and implemented SOA and ESB solutions in the late 1990's and 2000's were

---

[25] For about the first five years of Service-Oriented Architecture most practitioners pronounced the acronym "ess oh aye" and therefore the proper pronoun would be "an" as in "an SOA." Sometime in the middle of the SOA movement people started pronouncing it "sew-uh" and therefore would say they had "a SOA..."

ultimately disappointed. It was not so much that the products didn't work (most of them did). To get the benefit, firms needed to create a shared message culture; however, each application decided it was easier to publish their API to the bus and make everyone else deal with it, which ultimately lead to point-to-point interfacing over the bus.

In the end, SOA/ESB became eclipsed by the World Wide Web and RESTful endpoints.

AGILE

The agile manifesto turned the traditional waterfall methodology on its head. The waterfall method[26] as illustrated on the next page suggests that application development proceeds in a linear fashion from requirements to delivered product.

Installing loops in the process would make the outcome unpredictable, and un-schedulable. This is a derivative of the analogy between construction and software development. In construction, changing the location of the bearing walls halfway through the project usually has very severe cost implications. Software, done well, doesn't have the same downside. But because waterfall doesn't allow loops (they happen anyway, but that's a

---

[26] http://bit.ly/2j6PLdm.

different story), there is a premium on getting all the requirements up front.

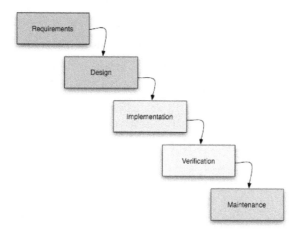

The agile approach embraces loops (iterations). See figure below.

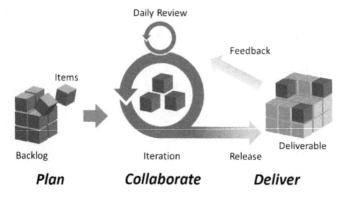

Agile Project Management: Iteration 27

---

27 http://bit.ly/1NLNXg1.

The agile approach says that encouraging users of the system to document all their requirements before a project starts (and informing them that this is the last shot they will get at them) encourages excessive over design.

These over-designed systems take far longer to build. Due to the large amount of time to implement these requirements, new requirements often pop up that cannot be ignored.

With agile, the users are encouraged to define a "minimum viable product" (MVP), that is some small subset of the final product features that they could begin to start enjoying benefit from. This MVP is the seed of the new system. The users can use the MVP and learn far more about what their real requirements are than when they were imagining them on paper.

We are big fans of the agile approach. We have embraced most of its components, including incremental building, test-driven development, pair programming, reducing technical debt, and continual refactoring.

Our observation is that agile has not addressed the core problem at large enterprises. While it makes individual applications smaller, more economical and easier to change (all of which are good things), it has not addressed the bigger picture of multiple, inconsistent applications and their databases.

If anything, it has made this problem worse. By encouraging small teams to solve individual problems, it fosters application proliferation.

An agile team will find a user story to implement. This inevitably involves persisting some data. They persist the minimum needed to solve the problem. In doing so, they have the "seed crystal" for another silo. As the team iterates on the business function they will add more and more data to the data store.

The problem is there is nothing impelling the developers to converge into a common model. If anything, the path of least resistance is more fragmentation.

Therefore, while agile has much to offer, left to itself it may be locally optimal and globally suboptimal. Our take is that many of the agile approaches need to be bolted on to a data centric, enterprise level approach.

DATA WAREHOUSE AND BUSINESS INTELLIGENCE

Up until the late 1980's if you wanted data or reports, you went to the application and used their reports or report writers. At some point, astute companies noticed that most information needs had to be sourced from many systems.

Hence the data warehouse was born. The basic ideas of a data warehouse were:

- A database could be built with a structure optimized for analytics

- The data warehouse could have a schema independent of any of the applications that fed it

- Many reporting needs were aggregations that could be pre-cached in the data warehouse to improve reporting performance

An industry was born. Complete with arguments: should we follow the Kimball method or the Inman method? Should we embrace "star schemas?" Should we load data marts into the warehouse or populate the data marts from the data warehouse? Should we have an "operational data store"?

What data warehouses did, that ERP and SOA did not, was combine data from many different applications and allow people to report against it. Ultimately, data warehouses sunk under their own weight.

In order to populate a data warehouse, you have to run programs that extract data from the source systems and conform it to the data warehouse schema. The process became known as ETL (Extract, Transform and Load for the three steps in the process). Several vendors (do you see a theme here?) stepped into the fray and provided ETL tools to ease the effort of writing these programs by hand.

However, the data warehouse came with many tradeoffs. The first was the data warehouse would contain only a small subset of the data from each application (the data of most interest for integrated reporting). Typically, this was the transactions such as sales orders, with the various ways of categorizing them such as by region, customer type, reporting period, and product type.

The second tradeoff was that the data warehouse would not originate transactions or updates of any type—it was for reporting only.

The third tradeoff was that the ETL process of conforming and populating the data warehouse was very analyst and developer intensive. This process required that an analyst learn enough about the source system that he or she could write a program to "extract" the information needed to populate the data warehouse. Inevitably, the data was incomplete and expressed in different terms than was needed for the warehouse. The "transform" portion of this process supplied missing data, conformed the source data to the target, and attempted to overcome problems with data quality. The "load" was merely a way to organize the posting of data to be as efficient as possible.

As more and more data was being extracted from the source systems to feed into the data warehouse, more and more tables were being created in the data warehouse. We have clients that have over 20,000 tables in their data warehouses. At some point this hardly seems like an improvement over just accessing the source files, other than in the process, the database access has been homogenized.

In a large organization, bringing a new data set to the data warehouse can often take months. The cost of change has gotten out of control and has led to the popularity of the "data lake", which we will discuss shortly.

OUTSOURCING AND OFFSHORING

The cost of professional services has come to dominant information systems costs. This has led to two reactions: outsourcing and offshoring. The two co-occur a lot and people have taken them to be synonymous.

Outsourcing is an attempt to change the incentives for professional services. When you hire people and pay them a salary, it is your problem to make them productive. Making IT people productive is notoriously difficult. Many business people have opted to pay for results, and make someone else responsible for getting the productivity. This is the essence of outsourcing: replace employment contracts with performance-based contracts.

Offshoring was the recognition that professional services, especially programming and testing, could be performed by people in countries that historically had much lower wages. Some firms hired their own employees in India,

China, Poland, Russia, and Bulgaria. Others allowed their outsourcing firms to do this. Either way, the basic economic idea was that if professional services were a large percentage of the overall cost structure of a firm's information system landscape, and if talented people in other countries were able to do the work for a fraction of the price, it should be possible to dramatically lower the costs by substituting the lower-paid professionals for the higher-paid ones.

OUTSOURCING

Many firms, frustrated by the growing diseconomy of their systems, and convinced that IT was not a core competency, were lead into the decision to outsource their IT departments wholesale.

While in theory this could have helped, in practice it made things worse. The outsource contracts reflected the diseconomy ("your mess for less" is how the saying went) but there were neither incentives to reverse this, nor incentives to improve the functionality of the systems. Most firms saw this as an opportunity to cut costs and not one to improve effectiveness, which they typically couldn't measure.

While it is hard to make people productive, it is also hard to come up with metrics that are representative and effective. Very often, an outsourcing contract recreated the same kind of economics, but with third party employees over whom you have even less influence. Moreover, while theoretically you could cancel one outsourcing agreement and replace it with another, from a practical standpoint there were many problems with this. The outsourcers were typically better negotiators, and usually negotiated very generous cancellation clauses, which meant that in effect it was harder to get out of an outsourcing contract than it was to fire a bunch of your own employees.

In many cases, the decision to outsource IT was borne of short-term economic hardship. A common outsourcing contract had the vendor make a one-time payment for the IT assets and staff, in exchange for a long-term contract. This provided a one-time boost to earnings and cash flow to the firm, but often ended up costing more in the long term.

Many outsourcing contracts have provisions for add-ons, but at prices pegged decades ago. One of our clients has an outsourcing contract that requires that all additional data storage be procured through and from the outsourcer, and that the equivalent of a small server will cost $20,000 / month. These were credible charges in the late 1990's but a small server can be deployed these days for about $100 per month, or in the cloud for $20 per month.

There is now a strong trend to "in source" or bring back into the fold the systems that had been previously outsourced, a clear indication that this trend did not solve the fundamental problem, and likely cost many firms several years of potential progress.

OFFSHORING

Offshoring hasn't worked out as well as firms intended. Most firms have discovered that the offshore workers need much more literal specs to be effective. There is something to be said for literal specifications; in some cases, this improves communication. For many types of systems, though, the cost to make the requirements literal is greater than the cost to implement. We're spending more money to get a watertight spec that can be implemented without error, than the original total cost would have been. This is masked because the cost of implementation has in fact gone down, if you only count the offshored component. However, in many cases, the total cost has gone up.

Additionally, many of the popular offshoring locations have been experiencing very high turnover. As members of India's technology class graduate into their first jobs with offshore companies, they rapidly develop marketable skills. This often leads to job-hopping. Turnover in Indian programming shops range from 25-40% per annum.[28]

We have several clients whose projects have been massively affected by the high turnover of their offshore IT groups.

---

[28] Employee Turnover in the Business Process Outsourcing Industry in India, in Management Practices in High-Tech Environments. Aruna Ranganathan (Cornell University, USA) and Sarosh Kuruvilla (Cornell University, USA) 2008.

This is not true in every case. We have known firms that have managed to get effective economics from offshoring some of their development and/or maintenance costs, but it is by no means an automatic saving, and it is typically far less than the wage differential by country. There is nothing about having your programming (or even design) done by lower cost workers that would lead to integration, and indeed everything about it that leads away from it.

This is true whether the offshored workers are your employees or whether they work for a contractor, systems integrator, or outsourcing firm. Separating the business needs from the implementers is making it less likely that a simpler solution will arise.

What we have seen is the focus on unit costs (labor costs for development primarily) tends to encourage more development (more modules, more lines of code) when a more economical architecture would have far less of both.

CLOUD

The cloud has changed the economics of deploying systems. For some reason this has caused some managers to believe this Holy Grail magically reduces all the related information systems costs. As we will see, some costs go down in a cloud environment, but not necessarily all costs, or even net costs.

Traditionally the cost to develop and the cost to implement a system were two of the largest costs in the lifecycle of an information system. In many cases the cost to maintain it over its life, while smaller on an annual basis often added up to more due to the life of the system.

However, cloud economics aren't about implementation or maintenance.

The cloud has brought us great economy, but it is primarily by reducing the cost of administering the servers.

As we mentioned earlier, the cost of hardware (the servers) plummeted in the 20th century. The same server processing power dropped in cost by over a million-fold. The cost to administer them barely moved at first and then picked up steam.

The cloud is about converting capital costs to expenses. In the old days, you might have to justify buying a mainframe computer or a large server to house your latest application. This was certainly several hundred thousand dollars and might be millions of dollars. This always had to go to the firm's capital committee. This always involved long delays, and questions about the return on investment.

Further, buying capacity meant buying more than you needed. You had to buy enough capacity to handle your peak need. Much of the time, you might be using far less than your peak. You were required to amortize the cost of the capital over the life of the system. The projections always called for level consumption of the resource throughout the life of the asset. In reality, though, projects were often delayed or only partially-implemented; this resulted in far less demand on the resource than predicted, but the business unit ended up having to cover the brunt of the expense.

Even without the capital committee, just getting another server procured and installed within a large firm was often a many month process. While not the dominant cost in the application cost structure, it was significant.

Administering servers means to take care of their procurement, installation, configuration, software installation, operation, maintenance, disposition, and replacement. As the cost of servers fell, the cost of administration per server rose. In the 1960's and 1970's several people were required to administer the mainframe computers that were the predominant servers at the time. By the 1980's with the advent of mini computers and later PC hardware based servers, one person could administer a server. By the 1990's administrators were managing dozens of servers. Through the 1990's and early 2000's that ratio kept changing. It had to. System Admins had to take care of more and more servers. For a while, the economics favored paying premium prices for larger servers (fewer to administer) and more reliable servers (breakdown maintenance costs a lot more than preventive maintenance).

Luckily, many technological and especially methodological advances were occurring that made the increase in the ratio possible. The rise of the web mega stars (Google and Amazon, as exemplars) showed how much more economical it was to buy unreliable and cheap rack-based servers, and build your system on the assumption that they would fail. Architectures were built around redundancy and fail over, and admins donned roller skates to patrol the vast datacenters to pick up and replace the failing components.

But the provisioning model kept moving on, and with the advent of Virtual Machines and Containers, the cost, especially the administrative cost, of spinning up another server, approached zero. We are now in an age of "server-less computers."

With all these changes, there are still hardware and networking costs, but these are now dispensed at the transaction and gigabyte level, rather than the capital expense of the network and the servers. Cloud expenses can be less expensive, can certainly be made to look less expensive, but at the end of the day you are still consuming CPUs, storage space, and network bandwidth.

Our contention is that while there have been terrific cost and resource improvements from going to the cloud model; they are a byproduct of wringing administrative costs out of the equations.

The rise of cloud computing was about being able to spin up a server in minutes (as opposed to months) and to pay only for what you used. If you were able to pay only for what you used, and contractually you could cancel at any time, you were able to put the costs in the department's expense budget.

However, think about this: what is letting everyone in your organization with a credit card and expense budget to become a systems implementer going to do to your overall systems architecture?

Each implemented cloud system has its own architecture. They all run on some operating system, they all have some storage model and products. They all have stacks of infrastructure and their own internal data models. This is making the cost of integration higher.

SOFTWARE AS A SERVICE (SAAS)

SaaS (and the "Cloud," more generally) reduces unit costs of infrastructure and makes spinning up more capacity more economical. However, if anything, they are making the integration problems worse.

Very often SaaS systems are implemented in cloud architectures. This means you need not implement a server, or a database or even any application code; you merely consume the functionality through a service. However, in order for a business application system to work, it must store information about clients, products, vendors, and orders for instance. This data is stored in the cloud, and implemented through a service interface.

Once apps become cheap enough that employees can put them on their expense reports, they will and they do. Imagine you have some employees with their contact information in salesforce.com, and others in Zoho, and still others in Microsoft Dynamics—you now have more integration points to contend with. The mere fact that data is in a SaaS vendor's database makes it far less likely that it is integrated with your data. The more this occurs the more pronounced the problem becomes.

Eventually the data in these cloud systems need to be integrated with other systems (including other cloud systems). They will need to be populated from other source systems. They will need to be kept in synch when things change elsewhere. They will need to publish the results of their activity to other systems that are interested but of course do not have the same data model.

The net/net of this is a brewing storm of "integration debt."

"Integration debt" is like technical debt, from the agile movement. In agile, *technical debt* refers to the inevitable entropy that results from evolving a system. It is usually easier to make a specific change by creating a "hack" that gets the immediate goal solved, but does so at the expense of the maintainability of the system overall. When people recognized that this happens all the time, they started calling it "technical debt." In agile, people often track the extent to which they are piling on technical debt and will occasional set aside sprints to address the technical debt, because they recognize that to postpone it too long will be to give in to the legacy forces which will ultimately lead to not being able to maintain it at all.

Integration debt is the practice of either not implementing needed integration or implementing it in a way that is not robust to change. Every time you implement a new system that has some overlapping functionality and therefore some data, with an existing system or systems, you have incurred integration debt.

Rampant implementation of application systems, in the cloud is resulting in a huge overhang of integration debt. The more we use Software as a Service (which is inherently not integrated) the more we are incurring integration debt.

DATA LAKES

Big data is primarily techniques borrowed from Google, Facebook and other early adopters of parallel processing against data sets that were too large to be processed sequentially. Many people think big data is the systems we have with more data. They think that a data warehouse with a petabyte of data is "big data." It is a lot of data, but big data is more a style of interacting with the data than an amount of data.

An idea that grew up with big data was the idea of "data gravity." Traditional systems move data from where it is, to a processor where it is processed and then some of it is written somewhere else.

At some point, the amount of data exceeds any reasonable bandwidth, and cannot be moved to the process. The data has enough mass (gravity) such that the code must go to the data not the other way around.

In big data environments, the data is spread over many machines. The algorithm to be applied is written in a way that it can be massively replicated. Each copy of the algorithm visits some subset of the data, extracts information, and returns to a predefined place where it can be combined with the results of the other copies of the algorithm to distill the answer. Because it is massively parallel, it can solve problems that couldn't be considered in traditional processing patterns.

One of the downsides is that all the set up and dispatching of the parallel algorithms and coordinating their partial answer adds considerable overhead, such that when people do proofs of concept projects with big data they are often disappointed. If you take a task that your system already performs and then try to do it with big data techniques, you often get slower results. This is because a problem you are already solving is within the boundaries of problems you can solve without big data, and using big data to address them is adding overhead where it isn't needed. Better to find some problem that is beyond what you can currently do.

Big data tended to favor problems that could be decomposed, such as looking for patterns in vast amounts of data.

Big data (and the rise of NoSQL) have given us, among other things the distinction between schema on write and schema on read. The distinction asks, in effect, "Do we need to have our entire schema in place before we write data to our database?"

Before the rise of big data, the distinction didn't make any sense. Your tables had to exist before you could write rows into them.

Schema on read says that although there may not be an explicit schema for the data, a competent data scientist can deduce schema on the fly ("on read") as they are processing the data.

The "data lake" approach took big data techniques and applied them to the frustrating parts of the data warehouse solution. Rather than conform the source data to the reporting structure, the data lake approach says, just lay the data down as it is. Then use big data techniques to find and correlate it at read time rather than at write time.

As it turned out, data warehouses were doing less and less conforming. In the early days of data warehouses, designers were careful to be economical about the facts they were storing in the data warehouse, and especially in being economical about reusing "conformed" dimensions. These days, data warehouses have thousands of tables, many of which resemble the tables of the applications they were extracted from.

Someone noticed that big data projects were dropping down external data in more or less whatever structure or format it was natively in. Why not do the same with our legacy systems? And so the data lake was born.

The data lake approach has the added benefit of traceability. Many firms are subject to Sarbanes Oxley requirements that firms be able to trace the lineage of the numbers that appear on their financial statements through the many systems that contribute to the calculation of the figure. Every transformation that data must go through becomes another link in a long chain that must be documented and managed.

This benefit is more a potential benefit than a real one though. So far, to the best of my knowledge, no firm is creating its financial statements from its data lake. Until they do, the traceability benefit will mostly accrue to internal data consumers, who seem to be more concerned with acquiring "insights" than in proving their provenance.

The essential tradeoff between a data warehouse and a data lake is between data acquisition and data retrieval.

Data Warehouse	Data Lake
High data acquisition (and conformance) costs	Low data acquisition costs, and minimal conformance
Low data retrieval costs (Business Analysts with Business Intelligence tools)	High data retrieval costs (Data Scientists with sophisticated statistics, AI and machine learning algorithms)

Some people have referred to the data lake as a "naïve data lake," and I would agree with that characterization. Most of the data lakes we are seeing now are naïve. There are many approaches to curate, organize, understand, and make data lake data more accessible to traditional analysis, but so far, these are mostly aspirational.

MACHINE LEARNING AND ARTIFICIAL INTELLIGENCE

Originally, AI (Artificial Intelligence) covered a wide range of programming that touched on almost anything that had previously been done by a human. Several decades in, many of the early AI sub disciplines are now disciplines in their own right: natural language processing, vision, rule-based systems, expert systems, planning systems, predictive systems, and goal driven systems.

Now the term AI is mainly applied to techniques where the intermediate mechanics are opaque. This line of inquiry started with neural nets and genetic algorithms. The current evolution is "machine learning."

The field of machine learning has settled into five major camps, each elaborating on a different core approach. The five camps are:

- **Inductive reasoning / symbolics.** Inductive reasoning is generally associated with rule-based approaches, where coding symbolic representation can lead to inductive conclusion of probable truth.

- **Connectionist / neural networks.** Neural networks attempt to mimic what we know about the self-organizing processes that go on in animal brains. The neural network postulates a series of intermediate layers that are connected to the inputs and outputs. Over time, "weights" in the intermediate layers begin to approximate our ability to form and use patterns in problem solving.

- **Evolutionary computation / genetic algorithms.** Genetic algorithms create a software analog to our genetic code. By defining a "fitness function," a system can randomly mutate the solution code and evaluate whether it maps to a more fit solution. By doing this millions of times over generations, these algorithms can often come up with novel solutions to complex problems.

- **Bayes Theorem / statistics**. Many machine learning algorithms at their heart are variations on Bayesian and other statistical methods applied to problems such as finding similarity in documents.

- **Analogical modeling / case-based**. Analogical modeling works from large numbers of cases, where the association between the provided input and desired output is ambiguous. That is, there is not a deterministic relationship between the two. Analogical modeling uses these cases as exemplars and works out the assignment of input to output.

Machine learning approaches are essentially black boxes. Today it is difficult to impossible to introspect the methods to determine why an algorithm provided a particular answer. While machine learning has many public successes, it still suffers from shortcomings such as overlearning, where the algorithm picks up on some non-important aspect of the input that was present in the training cases. The algorithm therefore can be fooled in ways that humans would not, such as in adversarial spoofing where a single changed pixel can cause an ML algorithm to misclassify something.

The black box nature of machine learning is problematic for many regulated industries, and has been criticized for recreating implicit bias that was in provided training sets.

Summary

When we began building enterprise application systems, computer hardware and network costs dominated the conversation and application projects were reasonable-sized projects that could be managed independently. Eventually as hardware and network costs plummeted, the cost of the application itself became the dominant cost, and most firms looked to licensed application systems to meet their business functionality needs.

However, eventually the number of applications implemented lead to a new problem becoming the economical dominator: the cost of integration. Integration now consumes most of large firm's information systems budgets.

Firms and vendors, have recognized the domination of integration as the driving cost, however the solutions mooted have done little to stem the tide. The idea that we could eliminate integration costs by implementing all functionality on a single, shared, relational model, ended up being an impossible dream.

SOA/ ESB and API driven architectures were meant to allow legacy and new systems to interoperate through a shared message model. However, while the infrastructure was implemented at some level in almost all large enterprises, the experiment was never completed, as virtually no firm was able to overcome the inertia of application developers putting their internal representation on the bus and forcing others to deal with it.

This is not without precedent. Brian Arthur in "The Nature of Technology," reminds us of the problems with changing technology ecosystems. By the mid 1800's the Industrial Revolution was running at full steam, literally. A typical factory of that era had a single large steam engine out behind the factory. The engine powered a shaft, which ran overhead into and through the factory to the far end.

THE SPINNING-ROOM IN SHADWELL ROPE WORKS.

The machines of the factory, the various lathes, drills, planes and the like were all driven from belts that descended from the spinning shaft at the top.

Toward the end of the 1800's electric motors had been invented. It was apparent to many people that electric motors would replace the steam and shaft style of factory design. This transition ended up taking over 50 years.

The first attempts at electrifying the factories tried to leave things much as they were. Electric motors were installed in place of the steam motors. As it turned out, though, electric motors (especially at that time) were not as powerful or as efficient as steam motors.

Where electric motors would shine would be when the motor was put in each device. What held the steam factories in place (in addition to their legacy entrenchment) was a subtle cross dependency of professions, trades, best practices, and habits. The experts of the day in factory design advocated methodologies that ensured that the workstations were aligned with the shaft and that the most efficient workflow was the one implemented. They were not interested in the flexibility that being able to move electric based workstations around provided. Architects who specialized in designing factories were the architects that knew about the stresses and loads a large spinning shaft would entail, and could architect a building to suit. Such a building would be over designed for electric manufacture. Therefore, a subtle combination of habit and precedence kept steam engines alive far longer than economically prudent. It is likely that the transition was not of firms switching, but more of firms going out of business, ultimately not being able to compete with the flexibility of the electric motors.

So it goes with application development and deployment. Despite the fact that the field is only 65 years old,[29] we have gone through many waves of technological advancement, each intending to revolutionize the economics of this business. Most have only had marginal impact, as we've seen.

After decades of reviewing progress, and especially lack thereof, in the world of application development and implementation, we have concluded that the root cause is not technological.

In the same way that it may have been obvious to some at the dawn of the electric age that this new approach would supplant the existing, the truth was that the status quo outlived its usefulness by many decades.

We owe it to ourselves to explore that habits of mind are keeping us mired in the quagmire.

---

[29] The first commercial software implementation was a payroll system for GE Sylvania in 1952.

CHAPTER 5
How we stay trapped

There are several self-reinforcing beliefs that are not true but continue to be believed. Many of these fallacies may have been true at some point, yet collectively they do far more harm than good.

1. "We need detailed requirements or we won't get what we want"
2. "It will cost more to reinvent the wheel"
3. "Software development is analogous to construction or manufacturing"
4. "Software projects can only be estimated by analogy"
5. "Having one neck to choke is an advantage"
6. "Each application has a positive ROI, therefore my IT portfolio must be returning far more than I am spending"
7. "We're not in the information systems business"

In the following sections, we will review where each of these ideas came from, what might have made them true at some point, why they are no longer true, and what we need to do to blunt their impact.

I have seen all of these. They often come up as clichés disguised as wisdom. One of the things that keeps clichés entrenched is the same as the dynamic behind generalizations. A generalization may be based on ignorance or a vast amount of knowledge. It may be based on flimsy association or rigorous scientific experiment. So, for instance if I were to say that "Kombucha causes kidney stones" you can't tell if this is the product of my association of the one time I drank Kombucha followed by the only kidney stone I've ever passed, or a double-blind experiment with testable scientific hypothesis involving a statistically significant population. All we can know for sure is that I will likely get a visit from the Kombucha lobby.

I bring this up because there is a meta-pattern behind these clichés that we need to be inoculated against. The people who perpetrate these clichés are often people with little or no experience in building or integrating the kind of systems we're talking about here. They are often in positions of influence or control over budgets and approaches. So often, right before you hear these fallacies declared, the speaker will wait for a pause in the conversation, and then with a studied flair, remove his or her glasses and set them down on the conference table and solemnly utter one of the seven fallacy clichés.

We need to keep our guard up. These fallacies are keeping us mired in a status quo that is slowly draining funds and energy. They are far more dangerous than they seem.

FALLACY # 1 "WE NEED DETAILED REQUIREMENTS OR WE WON'T GET WHAT WE WANT"

Once upon a time software was hard to change once built. Barry Boehm pointed this out in his classic Software Engineering Economics.[30] Studies of software development at NASA and defense contractors demonstrated that changing a function in a software system at the beginning of a project costs very little. There is no rework, since no work has been done.

Introducing a change at design time incurs additional cost, in particular if there is a great deal of design that must be redone to accommodate the change. Once coding starts, the cost of introducing a change starts to ratchet up rapidly. Again, if the change is introduced early in the code creating process, the impact is lower. Introducing a change late in the coding phase is very expensive, to the extent that it causes changes to other code.

Boehm's book was written in a time when most software was developed in a strict waterfall methodology, and

---

[30] Publisher: Prentice Hall; 1 edition (November 1, 1981) ISBN-10: 0138221227.

testing was generally not started until coding was complete. The cost to introduce a change to a function of the system once it has entered testing is often 10 times what the cost would have been had the change been introduced at the time of requirements gathering.

Finally, if the software is in use, in production, the cost of making a change explodes. 40 times is the figure often cited from these studies.[31]

Faced with this evidence, many prudent people collectively concluded that almost any amount of time spent in requirements would be worthwhile, as every function uncovered early would pay for itself 40 times over. Add to this the prevailing practices in most large firms and all government agencies of putting software out to bid. The scope of the project is the requirements that it must satisfy.

There is deep and long running truth behind the desire to produce detailed requirements before launching a software development project. Nevertheless, there is also a downside to this.

In the pursuit of completion, most projects dramatically over-specify their requirements. This has become more extreme in government agencies, largely because of their funding cycles. There are many state government

---

[31] http://bit.ly/2Bkb5Ee.

sponsored projects, where this excess is rampant. We will detail an example from Child Support Enforcement.

Child Support Enforcement is a relatively small agency in most states, and as such has more modestly-sized systems. Everything we will say about Child Support Enforcement is even truer for State Medicare and Medicaid systems, Department of Motor Vehicle Systems, Transportation Systems, State Patrol, Corrections, Employment Security, Pensions, and Education.

Every state has a Child Support Enforcement (CSE) system. Most were built in the 1970's or 1980's. Some are running on obsolete databases and programming languages. These systems have been inefficient for decades. The cost to make the simplest change is quite high. Most states soldiered on, though, as the capital costs to replace these systems was prohibitive. Eventually the cost and risk of continuing with the obsolete system motivate change, and a project is launched.

CSEs are mostly funded by the Federal Department of Health and Human Services (HHS). A state wishing to replace its aging system applies to the HHS for approval, and when the approval is granted, the state receives the assurances that it will be reimbursed 60-90% of the cost of the system.

The HHS, with most of the money on the line, wishes to ensure it is getting good value, and has created standard procedures and architectures that the states must follow. One part of this process is to perform a very detailed requirements analysis. These requirements studies typically take a year or more to complete, at costs of $5 million or more. In addition to interviewing all the personnel and reviewing the existing system in depth, the contractors who are preparing the requirements document have previous documents from other states to reference.

Each time a state initiates a project, the requirements get longer and more detailed. Although there is effort made to rank these requirements, each iteration just keeps getting longer, and including more "must have" requirements.

Armed with these requirements documents, the agency goes out to bid. "This is a complex system. Look at all these 'must have' requirements," say the bidders, and they bid accordingly.

We have been tracking these projects for about a decade (ever since we did a high-level design for the State of Colorado). Almost all the replacement projects done in the last decade have cost more than $100 million. Most go way over their original budget. Texas had a $200 million budget that ballooned to $300 million. They threatened to sue the contractor for breach of contract, but in the end asked the federal government for an additional $100 million to finish the project.[32] At $420

---

[32] http://bit.ly/2yIVxHh.

million it is now "back on track." California implemented their CSE for $1.7 billion.

The sad thing is that these replacement systems are scarcely better than the systems they replaced, in terms of cost to make subsequent change and cost to integrate with the state's other systems. These systems are no more prepared to transit off their database and language than their predecessors were.

Government projects of all sorts are famous for these types of excess. Consider the big dig in Boston or the Chunnel, each of which ran over their original estimates fivefold.

But the difference between millions of cubic yards of dirt and building a system to track deadbeat dads, is in the first case there is a real physical lower limit to what it could cost. In the latter case, the lower limit is approaching zero.

We know from our work with Colorado CSE, that a project well executed could be completed by a dozen people in less than two years. Some of this is by judicious use of agile technology, which we will cover subsequently. Some of it is through data centric design, which we will cover in the sequel to this book. But a great deal of it is just by replacing the detailed requirements, and the need to get it complete up front, with a system that prioritizes what it builds.

So while the fallacy is somewhat literally true: If you don't have detailed requirements, you won't get exactly what you want. The converse is even truer: your detailed requirements will drive your project costs up 10-100 fold, increase the risk, and greatly prolong the time taken.

It often costs as much to document "all" your requirements as it does to build a working version of the system. The big difference being if you build a system, you have something to work from, and your remaining requirements are clearer. If you write a multi-million dollar requirements document, you're pretty much committed to building an overly expensive system.

FALLACY # 2 "IT WILL COST MORE TO REINVENT THE WHEEL"

There is a great deal of truth to this cliché, which again is what makes it so persistent. As we will see, though, this has led many companies astray.

Who wants to reinvent the wheel? Why invent something that has already been invented?

But that isn't what this cliché is about in the business world. It is not about invention. It is really: "Why build what you could buy?" Here at the first level of approximation the answer should be "yeah, why would you build what you can buy?"

At the layman's level, you wouldn't build your own word processor or spreadsheet when they are readily available at modest prices. At the enterprise level, the decision gets murkier, and relying on metaphors from our personal buying habits may not serve us well.

Enterprise applications are expensive. Even the internal cost to procure them is expensive. We have had front row seats and watched several organizations spend years and at one organization spend over a decade trying to buy an ERP system. (Imagine what they could have accomplished in a decade if they hadn't been pursuing this goal.) As the price and the long-term commitment to a packaged application increases, so does the proportional internal cost of making the right choice.

However, it's not just the expense. As expensive as they are, few companies would believe they could recreate the functionality for less by building it or reusing existing well-tested components. Few companies would believe it, but this is what we are already seeing and will soon see more. The cost of creating and maintaining application functionality, if unmoored from proprietary legacy application packages, can be considerably more economical.

Before we elaborate on that claim, let's spend a bit more time on the hidden costs of application software acquisition.

The first hidden cost of application software is the annual license or maintenance fee. Recently this has been

ratcheting up to where it is often 20% of the purchase
price. Over a twenty year life, the annual maintenance
will be four times the original price, making the cost five
times the sticker price. Note that while a product you
build yourself will have ongoing maintenance, it will
mostly be features you actually want and/or adaptations
to your changing application landscape.

The second hidden cost to packaged applications is the
implementation cost. You might think that the cost to
implement a packaged solution and a custom solution
might be comparable, but they are not. I have had the
privilege of working on a custom system being
implemented in one division of a client while another
division was implemented a packaged solution. While the
packaged solution saved some money on development,
they more than made up for it in implementation. Let's
examine why this is so.

The cost of implementing a packaged application in an
enterprise is mostly driven by these activities:

- **Configuration.** As packages have become more
  and more complex, the act of turning on and off
  various features has become a dark art. In the
  world of health administration software, the
  battle between vendors is often pitched in the
  "how many flags do you have?" front. The
  "flags" are options you can turn on or off in the
  system functionality. These flags essentially turn
  on and off chunks of code within the system. In

some ways, configuration is the equivalent of coding. If there were just a few flags and they were isolated and independent, it would just be a matter of choosing between alternate bits of tested functionality. But when there are thousands, and they interfere with each other, configuration can get complex, and should only be performed by experts.

- **Modification or extension**. Most packages do not do exactly what you want them to. The alternatives are either to modify the software you've purchased or to extend with additional programs. Extension is greatly preferred because modifying third party code makes it very hard to stay current with package updates. However, often modification is the only way to go. Here we get an interesting bit of reuse of the concept introduced in the previous section. Recall that the cost of a change introduced late in a system's lifecycle can be 40 times as expensive as the same feature being introduced early in the lifecycle. Imagine you had 20 such changes you would want to introduce to a system. The cost of adding them to an already existing system would be 800 (40*20) times as much as adding them to a custom system early in its design stage. Keep in mind you still have to build the base system to apply the 20 changes, but as we'll see later, this is nowhere near as hard as it used to be.

- **Integration**. In most enterprises, the cost of integrating the new system with existing systems exceeds the cost of the system itself. The cost of integration is roughly proportional to the number of touch points in the enterprise, the number of touchpoints in the new package times the complexity of each, times each other. As mentioned in Chapter 1, the US Department of Defense gave up on their packaged HR implementation when the integration cost hit a billion dollars and was only one quarter complete.

- **Data conversion**. When you buy package software, you get a data model that is arbitrarily different from the one you are replacing. Also let's hope you are replacing only one, as many package implementations are additive: they are adding just a few extra features or datatypes that can't be handled by the existing systems, but aren't worth dismantling the existing systems. By itself, that isn't a problem. The problem arises when you do a trial conversion and you realize that in addition to being structured differently, the new system requires new data and has different ideas about data integrity and validation. This often gives rise to a "Data Quality" project to "Clean up" the data. Yes, your existing data had some weaknesses, but it mostly got the job done. The new system often has arbitrarily different ideas about quality (baked in from the vendors experience with other clients) that you must now conform. Again, the data clean-up project is often several times larger than the cost of the software. To be sure, some of the clean-up is useful, but most of the work is conforming to a different model.

- **Change management**. Most of your employees have grown up using the existing system. This is how they know your business and your industry. Whatever the labels are on the screens and reports, whatever workflow the system has imposed on them, over time becomes their internal mental model of how a system should work. Many have made careers out of working around the idiosyncrasies in the existing system to get it to work. The new system has all new screens, new reports, new terms, new labels, new implicit and explicit work flow, and a need for a whole slew of new workarounds. The new system proclaims this state of affairs as "best practice." It is just some averaging of the vendors' original conception with whatever part of their implementation experience they could fit back into the base product. There is occasional streamlining. However, the jarring nature of the change leads to a need for "change management," which is a euphemism for retraining people who had learned on the job and aren't excited about a system that typically isn't easier, just different.

Again, the change management portion of a package implementation project can easily exceed the cost of the system.

Early in my consulting career, we often selected and implemented packaged solutions for clients. Many of those worked out well. However, part of this was due to the relative simplicity of the systems in those days, and part was due to how few other systems there were to integrate. Furthermore, another part of it was that people were coming from no system to a system, rather than from system to system. The manual data entry of the master files was both data conversion and training all in one.

Now the landscape has changed. I remember as packages started getting more complex in the early 1980's sitting in on a pitch by a consulting firm to do a packaged implementation, and how they explained that the cost of implementing this type of system was typically three times the software acquisition cost. I would sit in on many more of these types of pitches over the years, and the multiplier climbed from three to five to ten. I'm not even sure what it is anymore.

However, even in that first meeting it struck me: what, if any, is the relationship between the professional services needed to implement a package and the cost of the package?

This thinking still prevails.[33]

I had a flashback to one of my first professional jobs, as a real estate agent for a company that specialized in selling taverns. I had just turned 21, and looked about 16, which made it difficult for me to get into the taverns to ask if the proprietors would like to list their establishment for sale with us. What I struggled with more than my youthful appearance was this firm's approach to valuation. The owner of the realty firm had decided that a Tavern should sell for about $10,000 times the number of kegs they went through per month.

I was a business major at the time and this made no sense to me. It seemed to make sense to everyone else, because after a decade or so of promoting this idea, whenever I'd show someone a tavern and want to go over its P&L they would ask how many kegs they went through in a month and decide the price was either high or low. A tavern could be losing money, and gaining value based on the number of kegs they went through. It certainly discouraged ancillary activity such as food, wine, or liquor that typically have much higher margins but don't contribute to the keg metric.

I saw the implementation metric the same way. What possible connection could there be? If the software company suddenly charged half their previous fee, would the consulting magically drop in half? No, I saw only two

---

[33] http://bit.ly/2ADGwIx and http://bit.ly/2kz4Lkm.

correlations. First, over time, the four cost drivers of package implementation kept climbing. Second, software that was more expensive tended to be more complex, and complexity is a prime contributor in all four of the above cost drivers.

Finally, each package (really each application, but packaged applications are both more numerous and more complex) adds to the overall entropy of the enterprise. An enterprise with 10 major application systems is a bit complex and it will take effort to introduce an 11th application into that mix. However, introducing the same application into an enterprise with 100 or 1000 applications is much more difficult, and each application added to the mix raises the cost for all subsequent applications.

We've laid out the many hidden costs of packaged implementations, but this still doesn't necessarily make them more expensive than their custom alternatives. We have just seen that the total cost of implementing and owning a package application is often 10-20 times its purchase price, meaning that it is incumbent on us to look very hard at the build versus buy decision before retreating to simple clichés.

The agile software industry has pretty much proven empirically what I'm suggesting here logically. It is often much cheaper and faster to build functionality than to buy it.

WHEN YOU SHOULD BUY PACKAGED SOFTWARE

You should buy packaged software when:

- You can use it as is with no modification and simple customization

- It contains internal logic that far exceed your own organization's ability to develop

- It has simple or uniform interfaces that could be made to conform to your firm's data model, rather than forcing you to adopt yet another variation

- The purchase price is at least ten times less than your estimate of what it would cost to build the functionality in house

- You have real time pressures that would mean the time to implement would be a key factor in an implementation. However, while the cost of development adds time to your timetable, you may gain it back with reduced time to implement.

WHEN YOU SHOULD BUILD SOFTWARE

There are two scenarios for opting for the build route:

- The small application
- The many large applications

An example of a small application problem is automating some low volume or low complexity business area for your firm. Maybe you want to automate the supply rooms in your offices or employee progress on a training curriculum. These are projects where your needs and requirements are often modest.

If you have even a very small band of agile developers, you'd be surprised how quickly they can create a first working version of these types of systems, and how rapidly they can iterate toward a completed state.

The "many large applications" scenario is much more nuanced. When you have many large (legacy) systems, it is tempting to want to upgrade them. "Legacy modernization" is the current term of art for replacing your legacy systems with neo-legacy systems. Neo-legacy systems are systems that are built with more modern programming languages, databases and the like, but which none-the-less have most of the undesirable features of the original legacy systems such as high cost of change.

When you have dozens of legacy systems, it is tempting to try to knock them off, one at a time. There is a very important flaw in this thinking. The boundaries of what is in one application or another are not logical. They are based on the sequence of events that led to this particular configuration of applications. Even two firms with the same applications will often use them for different subsets of their business, purely for reasons of historical accident.

If you are committed to getting out of the application quagmire, it will require some strategy and at least some custom development. You will need a long-term plan that allows you to build new functionality that partially relies on your new more permanent and stable data structures and partially reaches into your existing systems for functionality and data you haven't had time to convert yet. As you can probably appreciate, this kind of functionality is almost the opposite of packaged application functionality. It is about lightweight functionality riding lightly and changing frequently.

If you are in this situation, we recommend two sub strategies with regard to build versus buy:

- The functionality that you will need to bridge the new with the old will be mostly built. You may buy an architecture or environment that makes it easier to build this, but the combinations you have to construct have never been encountered before, and are de facto custom.

- When you get ready to tackle a component that has the potential to be a package, estimate what it would cost to custom build the functionality you need before you go out to bid. Take an Accounts Receivable system for instance. There is very little logic in an AR system. Aging of receivables is just categorizing based on due date versus todays date. Calculating late fees and early payment discounts are just a few simple rules, based on balances and cutoff dates. Recurring invoices reuse templating and scheduling features. Most of the rest of the functionality is records management and form population. If you're still on the fence, have one of your agile teams build a MVP (minimum viable product) prototype of the needed system. You will know in less time than it takes to launch an RFP whether they will rapidly converge on the features you need or not.

In my opinion the build/buy decision, whether for a small standalone application or as an overall modernization strategy, deserves a great deal more thought than just throwing out the cliché "Let's not reinvent the wheel."

FALLACY # 3 "SOFTWARE DEVELOPMENT IS ANALOGOUS TO CONSTRUCTION OR MANUFACTURING"

Once upon a time writing software was an art form, more akin to poetry than engineering. However, things got big and complex and eventually the engineering analogy took hold. In general, this was a good thing. As systems became larger, more discipline was needed. Along the way, though, another analogy took hold. This one was aided and abetted by the Zachman Framework:[34]

---

[34] Data Management Body of Knowledge 2nd Edition, DAMA International, Technics Publications, page 103.

	What	How	Where	Who	When	Why	
Executive	Inventory Identification	Process Identification	Distribution Identification	Responsibility Identification	Timing Identification	Motivation Identification	**Scope Context**
Business Management	Inventory definition	Process Definition	Distribution Definition	Responsibility Definition	Timing Definition	Motivation Definition	**Business Concepts**
Architect	Inventory Representation	Process Representation	Distribution Representation	Responsibility Representation	Timing Representation	Motivation Representation	**System Logic**
Engineer	Inventory Specification	Process Specification	Distribution Specification	Responsibility Specification	Timing Specification	Motivation Specification	**Technology Physics**
Technician	Inventory Configuration	Process Configuration	Distribution Configuration	Responsibility Configuration	Timing Configuration	Motivation Configuration	**Tool Components**
Enterprise	Inventory Instantiations	Process Instantiations	Distribution Instantiations	Responsibility Instantiations	Timing Instantiations	Motivation Instantiations	**Operational Instances**
	Inventory Sets	**Process Flows**	**Distribution Networks**	**Responsibility Assignments**	**Timing Cycles**	**Motivation Intentions**	

The analogy is this: construction and manufacturing take designs and turn them into real things.

In the case of construction, there are generally blueprints but often not to an extremely precise level of detail. House blueprints generally specify where walls are but not where the nails go. Manufacturing often specifies the build process in detail but this is in order to make the exact same thing repeatedly. Perhaps the best analogies and the ones that got used the most, were those for products that combine many features of construction and manufacturing: aircraft and submarines.

Here is how the analogy works.

A complex thing, like an airplane or a submarine, starts life as a conceptual design. The design is gradually transformed from one rendition to another, each at a greater level of detail and precision. At each level, different constraints apply. In the airframe business, this high-level design is called the "air transport system," which determines if the design is feasible (Can it fly?) and if we have the right features (Are customers more interested in range or fuel efficiency?). There is no point investing engineering time on detailing features that won't work or aren't wanted.

The second level in the airframe business is called the industrial process. At this point, they work out issues like the propulsion system, level of technology and risk, and key suppliers and partners. There are design decisions made at this level, including preliminary materials selection and more elaborate designs.

The third level in airframe design is the engineering level. At the airframe design level, the design splits into many specialized sub disciplines, each of which creates a more detailed model, subject to their own constraints, and then the various models are reintegrated. This is also the level where the direct operating costs are established.

The fourth level is subsystem design where all the subcomponents are optimized.

In the software analogy, Zachman has proposed six levels:

- Executive Perspective (scope)
- Business Management Perspective (business concepts)
- Architect Perspective (systems logic)
- Engineer Perspective (technology physics)
- Technician Perspective (tool components)
- Enterprise Perspective (operational instances)

Across each of the levels there are six "interrogatives" (what, how, where, who, when, and why) that further subdivide the subdomains of interest.

While this was originally justified as an analogy to other complex construction / manufacturing process, the analogy seems to breakdown in many ways.

Firstly, while it is inescapable that design changes late in the manufacturing or construction process have huge cost impacts (it's pretty easy to move a bearing wall before a building is built, it very costly to do so after the building is built). And while early generation software had many of these same characteristics (expensive to change in the field), modern distribution methods coupled with agile development methods mean that changes can be propagated late in the delivery process. Amazon can roll out a system change in minutes. Amazon has gotten so good at continuous deployment, they are now rolling out five changes to their production systems per second.

Now that the cost of change has been changed so profoundly, we recognize that the basis for the analogy of software to construction has completely broken down. Airplane designs are on paper or electronic, but the planes are made of aluminum (and other materials). However, with software there is no such materiality shift. Today designs are electronic artifacts as is the final system. As such, there is no essential need to transform from level to level.

In the old days, there was no way to implement a conceptual model, so it seemed natural to think this was an initial phase in the design of the system. In the same fashion, logical models were not directly implemented and table and column names were changed as the design became more physical. Indexes and other implementation considerations were introduced at the bottom of the matrix.

In systems built from architectures like this (including TOGAF, which is an open standard based architecture), there is a tendency for the conceptual models to get left behind. If you create a conceptual model and then derive a logical model from it, in the process you will learn new things and alter your logical model. It is a great deal of extra work to go back and keep the conceptual model up to date. This can be somewhat alleviated if the logical model can be completely created from the conceptual model, but if this is possible, you should ask yourself if there is a need for two models. In any event, in our observations conceptual and even logical models are rarely kept up to date with the conceptual and logical models that spawned them.

In our opinion, the separation by level is an artifact of older design techniques that actually hampers application development.

In software, the artifacts at the conceptual level can be the same as those at the implementation level, such as with more modern databases like graph and document.

The analogy breaks down further in that software and data are reusable in ways that physical things are not. If you decide that an airplane should have two engines, you aren't done when you've built one engine. However, in software if two processes need one shared routine, the second one is complete when the first one builds the routine.

The interrogatives are semantic distinctions, to be sure, but in an information system, they all end up as data. There is essentially no cost to reusing software. There is data about the:

- what (physical things)

- how (process templates and process instances)

- where (at one level geospatial location of the physical things and at another the geospatial location of the data centers and data itself)

- who (identification and in some case authentication of individuals referred to or participating in the system)

- when (the framework focuses on cycle time, but other temporal aspects are important such as temporal relationships)

- why (goals and metrics are the data instantiation of motivation)

So it's all data—different types of data. There is data about types of items (e.g. Employees and Patients) and there is data about individual things (e.g. Nurse Nichols and Jeff). Most of the type information may be developed "higher" in the framework, and most of the individuals come into existence after the system is put into practice.

We see little value in sticking with this analogy. It encourages a multitude of models, when a few will do. It encourages transformation, when sub-setting will do. It encourages new identifiers when the concepts and identities have not changed.

We have found that abandoning this analogy allows us to build conceptual models and then populate and use them. There is something akin to levels, but there is no need to have transforms between them. When we want to change an implementation, we change the configuration at the implementation level. If it involves something at the conceptual level, we introduce that at the conceptual level and it is immediately available at the implementation level, no need for transformation. We will pursue this in more detail in the companion book.

Overall, we find that this analogy hampers rather than helps the development of systems.

FALLACY # 4 "SOFTWARE PROJECTS CAN ONLY BE ESTIMATED BY ANALOGY"

After abandoning the construction or manufacturing analogy for software building, you may think it odd that we embrace it for estimating.

Let's retrace the history of software estimation to see how we got to where we are. What we will see is that for the most part, software project estimates have been getting larger for the same functionality, at the same time that they are getting less accurate.

Early on, people had no idea how long it would take to write and debug a program. Luckily, over time people ended up writing programs that were incredibly similar, and it became like a craft industry. In a craft industry, once you know how long it will take to form, fire, glaze, seal, and finish a bowl, you can pretty well estimate how long it will take to do the next one. You might make adjustments for necks, handles, and lids, but you will have a base estimate with parametric adjustments.

It was in the craft stage of software development. Once you had written the inventory receipt program, you had a good idea how long a cash application program was going to take. In those days, and even today, few people understand that this is the same program, and are happy to be craftspeople and knock out lots of similar pieces of art that are hand crafted, and only slightly different one from another.

At this point some project manager tired of overseeing a group of craftspeople whose output he or she couldn't predict or manage, decided to start measuring and predicting. The first attempts focused on the output. This is a reasonable approach if you are going to measure ditch diggers or tailors. You might measure cubic yards of trenches, or linear feet of seams sewn. However, this approach falls down in other domains. Measuring light by wattage is such an example, as long as all light bulbs were equally inefficient we could correlate light (luminosity) with power consumption (wattage). With compact florescence and LEDs, that correlation is out the window. Similarly, if we measured our potters by the pound I could guarantee that we would have many larger and heavier bowls.

LINES OF CODE

This was also the case with software. The primary early metric was LOC (lines of code). The belief was that a program twice as long must have solved twice as difficult a problem. Moreover, a project manager could estimate how large their system was (in LOC) and measure progress toward that goal.

Only this backfired massively. Once programmers knew they were being measured by LOC, they started writing more and more LOC. Reusing a subroutine was detrimental to getting credit for writing more lines. I recall watching project managers recoil in horror as their LOC counts exploded and the project hardly moved any closer to completion. The number of lines of code continued to grow, actually harming productivity.

While the number of lines of code is barely correlated with the size of the problem being solved, it is highly correlated with something else: defects.[35] Different industries and different development approaches lead to different defect rates, but there are patterns:

- There are inherent defect introduction rates. These range from about 1-3% of all human decisions

- Defects can be introduced in any phase of the development process (requirements, design, coding)

- Most software defects are found before product release

- Different development styles (for instance coding with complex conditional branching logic) introduce defects at different rates

- Different defect detection methods (testing, inspection, etc.) have different discovery rates

One thing they all converge on: the more code you write, the more bugs you produce. From the studies that I have

---

[35] http://bit.ly/2Cq5tYx.

reviewed, the number of latent bugs in released software ranges from 1 per KLOC (thousands of lines of code) to 15 per KLOC. Your program with a million lines of code has at least a thousand defects. Unless you have a particularly rigorous defect detection method, you may have 15,000 defects in your released product.

If you allow or encourage your developers to solve the same problem with more lines of code, not only are you ruining their real productivity (while enhancing their perceived productivity), you are increasing your defect rate. Let's say you have a latent defect rate of 1% (10 defects per KLOC). If you have a problem that could have been solved with 1 million lines of code, you should expect to ship it with 10,000 defects. If that doesn't bother you, consider if your perverse incentive program of rewarding line of code production actually "worked." Imagine you solved the same problem with 2 million lines of code. For the sake of argument, let's say your incentive systems resulted in twice the "productivity." You would be done at the same time with a system that now has 20,000 defects. Of course, if you actually did achieve twice the average daily output of code per developer, you should expect an even higher defect rate – "haste makes waste" as they say.

This is not a theoretical concern. Anyone who delivers software knows that these defects come back to haunt.

As such, a line of code turns out to be not a very good metric for estimating project size, but a very good metric for measuring defects. Hold that thought for later fallacies.

FUNCTION POINTS AND USER STORIES

It is much more productive to size the problem, rather than size the solution. The function point methodology does this by assigning points to various aspects of the problem to be solved. There are points for interactive forms, more points for more fields and more complexity. There are points for interface transactions, point for reports, and points for tables and columns.

What is important is there aren't function points for lines of code. In fact, it flips the productivity question on its head and allows you to ask: How many lines of code did it take to build this? It allows you to compare programming languages for their productivity.

Here is an excerpt from a study by QSM on the average number of lines of code per function point for different programming languages:[36]

Language QSM SLOC/FP Data			
Avg	Median	Low	High
ABAP (SAP) * 28	18	16	60
ASP* 51	54	15	69
Assembler * 119	98	25	320
Brio + 14	14	13	16
C * 97	99	39	333
C++ * 50	53	25	80
C# * 54	59	29	70
COBOL * 61	55	23	297

[36] http://bit.ly/2omnlkO.

It expresses what we would expect: some programming languages are more expressive, and therefore encourage writing more functionality with fewer lines.

The agile movement has done something even more upstream: estimation by user stories. A user story is a narrative description of a problem to be solved. Team members consider the size, complexity, and risk of the request, relative to where the product is at that time, and create subjective estimates of "points" per user story. There is no uniform definition of the size of a story point or the amount of time a given team will take to develop it, but most teams converge on consistent values for both the points and their velocity. Velocity is the agile term for the rate at which you turn user stories into tested software.

Both function points and story points have been proven accurate ways of estimating software development projects. However, this is not how most large software development projects are estimated.

DETAILED WORK PLANS

Another approach to estimating is to prepare a detailed work plan of all the tasks needed to complete the project. While it has the look of a metric-based estimate, it mostly is judgement-based, relying on the estimator's judgment about the size of each of the tasks.

I remember one of my first major projects was to do a high-level design of a custom payroll system for a large forest products company, and to then estimate the cost to build and implement said system.

This was just before spreadsheet software was invented, and so the work plan was handwritten on dozens of large format manual spreadsheets. I remember sitting down with my boss to review my estimates before we presented them to our client. There were hundreds of tasks. He started with some of the first ones and challenged my estimates: "80? No I think we can do this considerably faster than that, let's say 30." Then on to the next one. "240? Let's make it 150." On it went for another ten minutes or so, until we got to one that I couldn't see cutting, and I protested. "There is no way we could complete that task in 10 hours." "10 hours? I thought these estimates were in days."

That says a lot for subjectivity in estimating. Even detailed task level estimates. And for anyone who has ever had to manage to these "estimates," you realize that what you actually do in the project bears only a remote relation to the original work plan.

ESTIMATION BY (GROSS) ANALOGY

The subjectivity just ramps up as the scale ramps up. My observation is that large IT projects are estimated by analogy. The large systems integrators that have done "similar" projects, size up the gross characteristics of the system such as size of the client, number of employees affected, and number of systems to be integrated, and then rely on their experience with similar projects to provide estimates.

It is great that they have experience, but this experience is impossible to challenge or question, or even quantify or qualify. Generally, the reasoning is something like "we did a similar project for another company in this industry, and it took three years and cost $100 million, yet we lost money on that project so we should bid this at $120 million." I've done estimating and therefore I know there is more behind their estimates than this, and there is always a work plan behind the estimate but it is more difficult to justify the effort than determine it.

I was recently on a raft trip with the manager of a large (100,000 employees) second-tier consulting firm. He was relating the difficulty there were having in convincing a client that they were the right firm for an $800 million customer support systems project. They had only ever done a $200 million customer support project. He was worried that the client would be swayed to go with a tier 1 firm that actually had experience with such scale projects. The real question is this: How did the client (and the consultants) become convinced that this was an $800 million project? Because once convinced, it is a self-fulfilling prophecy.

Although I haven't seen the justification for the $800 million customer support project, I suspect based on project work ups I've reviewed that substantiation will be in a very voluminous report, with scores of Excel spreadsheets, and will appear to be very detailed and authoritative. In the cases where I have dug in deep, I've found that often most of the estimate is based on a few very high level assumptions, which are then extended, multiplied and variously factored up to get the detailed work plans (almost always with two or three alternative approaches that have been similarly grossed up for comparison). The human mind does better with relative amounts than absolute amounts, so when you put an $800 million project plan up against the alternative approach which is $925 million, the $800 million wins every time.

In addition to the contribution to project inflation, the other difficulty with this type of estimate is that it is completely unhelpful in making any kind of decision on course of action as the project is progressing.

I once reviewed the detailed justification for a packaged implementation for a state agency. The key part of the spreadsheet consisted of 150 rows and 17 columns (mostly out year projections). However, if you drill down on many of the key cells in the spreadsheet, they eventually traced back to a couple of numbers far off to the right on the spreadsheet and out of sight to most anyone reviewing the analysis. These two numbers were the cost to upgrade the current system ($84 million) and the cost to implement an ERP system ($115 million). There was no other source for these numbers, and the rest of the spreadsheet just allocated and spread these numbers around by year and by expense category. We were working on another project in parallel, and had an opportunity to review our own estimates of the project with some knowledgeable stakeholders. Our back of the envelop estimate was that the implementation would be closer to $1 billion than $100 million. The stakeholders concurred. In the ensuring 10 years the project has still not been attempted, so we'll have to wait to see whether the precise but spurious estimate was correct or the back of the envelop one.

SUMMARY OF ESTIMATION

Unless you have a way to estimate the cost of introducing a new function or feature to your system, you will have no basis for making decisions. You will have no way of evaluating your contractor. You will discover way after the fact that "this was way harder than we thought."

There are ways to describe the functions you are loading on to your system. There are ways to prioritize them. There are ways to evaluate whether a given team is more or less productive than another.

You need to embrace these methods and turn your back on megaproject estimation, which never reveals any low-level quantification of the basis of the estimates (other than experience). If your contractors are basing their estimates on their experience, and are not managing against anything that will get better over time, their estimates and productivity will continue to get worse over time.

FALLACY # 5 "HAVING ONE NECK TO CHOKE IS AN ADVANTAGE"

We hear this often. This comes from the experience of hiring several consulting firms to solve a problem, and then having them blame each other for problems on the project.

One analogy may be your basement remodel. You could hire an architect to design the space, a plumber to redo the bathroom and plumb in the sink, a cabinet maker for the cabinets, tiler for the shower and backsplash, carpet layer for the floor, and select all your fixtures and appliances yourself. You have some choices as to how to coordinate this. You could be the project manager yourself. This is mostly a question of time and inclination. You can hire a general contractor, who will coordinate the subcontractors but who isn't liable for their work, or you can hire someone to do the whole thing.

A basement remodel is pretty tangible and easy to imagine the tradeoffs on the management models. Having just completed a basement remodel, let me share my assessment. Our project cost about $50,000. About half was materials, about a third was various skilled and unskilled laborers, and about 1/6 was for the general contractor (we went with the middle model).

We opted to have the concrete floor ground and stained. When the floor contractors screwed up, our general helped us hold their feet to the fire, but there was never any question as to whose fault it was and whose responsibility. We were not going to require the general to redo their work.

In the "one neck to choke" model, we would have said: "You're responsible for everything, hire whichever subs you want, but you have to make good." I'm sure, had this been an option, the price would have ballooned. First, the general is only going to hire the best contractors (can easily get cost inflation here), is going to pad the estimate to make sure they can handle any claims, and will be very rigorous about the scope.

My guess is this sort of arrangement could have easily doubled the cost of our basement project. The cost gets away from you because there is no inbuilt market for each part of the project. The way we did it, we could cost different concrete treatment subcontractors, and if that looked like it was getting unreasonable, we could shift to wood or carpet. Once you go for an all-in price, you lose a lot of the opportunity for constructive change.

Unlike a basement project, if you're launching a systems project, you have no idea how much it will cost. My observation is getting a sole source for a large project is almost guaranteeing it will cost five to ten times what it would cost if it were more proactively managed.

J. Paul Getty once said:

*If you owe the bank $100 that's your problem. If
you owe the bank $100 million, that's the bank's
problem.*[37]

This analogy is apt for large projects. If you are a
hundred million dollars into a hundred and ten million
dollar project, it is your problem and not the problem of
your contractor.

There may be some comfort in knowing whose neck it is
you want to choke, but the actual likelihood of getting
anything from your choking effort is slim.

Before you settle in on a "one neck" contracting strategy,
think through what each aspect of your system could
cost, if it were done using modern approaches and
contractors who were not incented to pad the bill.

We like to start this thought process two ways. One is to
decompose the work into chunks that can be considered
independently (like the floor and the cabinets in the
basement project analogy) and then to consider what
best cases and worst cases look like for each.

Most system implementation projects involve:

- **Application software (buying, building, adapting,
  etc.).** Sometimes it helps to decompose the
  problem a bit, as some of the parts are easier to
  think about independently. The Child Support
  Enforcement system I mentioned earlier

---

[37] http://bit.ly/2AGpPfD.

decomposes nicely into four major sub systems, each of which is quite different, and might be better addressed with different types of technology. There is an intake portion, which is very similar to most case management systems and is primarily a workflow and form filling system. There is a financial system, including transactions, audit trails, and reconciliations, in place to prove that all funds were dispersed according to policy. The remedies sub system is mostly about rules (how many days' notice is given before you revoke someone's chauffeurs or hunting license) and external interfaces (how you automate the sending of the license revocation to the appropriate agency). Finally, there are business intelligence / analytics functions that need to be addressed. When you divide it up like this, it's much easier to estimate and to know what you need to create an adaptable system.

- **Data**. There is usually data to convert, data to acquire, data to create, and often data to clean up. It is possible to sample your data well ahead of time to get an idea of the overall quality and appropriateness of your data and the effort it will take to prepare it for the new system.

- **Processes**. New systems often involve changing to established processes. The general errors that people make in estimating these are:

o   Underestimating the time and cost for your users to learn the new system. The larger the workforce affected the more time should be spent making the system intuitive, rather than relying on training to make the transition.

o   Being overly optimistic that the users will accept the changed processes. Often the new system proposes changes that the users are either actively or passively opposed.

o   Too much detail in proposed process flows. Designers often believe they can and should flow chart out every possibility and train people for them. While this sounds like a good idea, it can easily get out of hand, and many hypothetical special processes get designed and built that aren't necessary or are so rare as to not warrant codifying.

- **People.** Some systems require people to obtain new skills or learn new approaches. These are hard to estimate and should be decoupled from implementation. For instance, if I were to redo an airlines internal system, I would create a system flexible enough to mimic the existing system (with all the keyboard shortcuts and manic typing), and in parallel introduce more intuitive, graphic, drag and drop interfaces. Although it would cost more, it would take the massive retraining off the critical path for the project, and allow it to come in a much more phased approach.

When you've chunked the main portions of your project into the above buckets, start thinking about what each is likely to cost and how long it's likely to take. I like to think about cost of each chunk in three ways:

- Would cost
- Should cost
- Could cost

WOULD COST

In this breakdown, "would cost" is what you would expect to pay if you let things go their normal route. "Would cost" is what you'll get if you go with the "one neck" theory. If you bring in consultants to estimate project costs, they will base their estimates on analogies to other projects they have done. These are almost always analogy estimates and not parametric estimates.

We work a lot with a state agency who had contracted a firm to estimate the cost of an ERP implementation. After surveying a number of states, they came up with the number $125 million +/- $20 million.

Our independent assessment, based on other work we had done for this agency and our knowledge of the scope suggest that a realistic range of costs for the project ranges from $5 Million to $1 Billion +. As strange as it sounds, both of those extremes are as likely as $125 million. Actually, they are more likely. As we'll discuss, the $125 million number (even with the +/- $20 million) is almost impossible to hit.

The problem with a $125 million project is that you staff up for it. Most companies don't have the resources to staff a $125 million project, so they go outside. Consultants may add some additional software to the total, but it's hard to spend much more than a few tens of millions on software. The real purpose of adding software to an implementation project is to give the staff something to do.

External consultants typically charge $150-$200 / hour or about $300K - $400K per year. You'll need 300-400 person years to hit a $125 million budget. It's just not possible to get that many people coordinated around a one-year project—it will be 3-5 years, with 100 people.

100 people trying to solve a complex, highly interconnected problem usually end up in the same place: a certain percent of the team are discovering the "real" requirements (which changes work done to date) and another percent are uncovering new constraints (many from the software that was selected to try to solve the problem). This effort, while well intentioned causes churn on the work done to date. No one wants to admit that this is happening until it is too late to deny it.

By this time, it's time to re-baseline the project.

Why do I say it's just as likely to hit either extreme? At the high end you have only to look at Healthcare.gov, the California Child Support Enforcement System, or the DOD DIMHRS system to see how medium-sized systems projects can easily become billion-dollar blowouts.

Most of these systems are not complex. A team could tackle the whole thing in an agile fashion and be done in a fraction of the time and cost.

Therefore, "would cost" is if you accept the advice of the "best practice" practitioners, budget $100 million and spend $200 million.

SHOULD COST

Decomposing the project into its chunks allows to you start thinking about "should cost." "Should cost" is what it would cost you if you knew before you started most of the problems that were going to cause the prices to balloon, and addressed them proactively. This is the cost if you used traditional technology and executed as well as possible. Let's say we used case management software for the intake portion of the child support system discussed earlier, a simple accounting system for the financial distributions, and some flexible rule and integration system for the enforcement part, it's not hard to imagine each of these sub-projects being less than $20 million and far less risky.

COULD COST

The "could cost" goes one step further. If you knew what was likely to change the most (forms and therefore database structure in the intake, allocation rules in the financial system, and legislated law about notification in the enforcement side), you'd lean toward approaches that made those kinds of changes easy. In the same way that Amazon has streamlined their cost of introducing changes to their online sales system, your cost analysis should focus on architectures that make the parts of the system you will have the most components, variation, and change to the easiest.

If you knew that the cost driver would be the number of interactive User Interfaces (UI) that needed to be built, instead of rolling up your collective sleeves and coding them, you asked "What would need to be true to get the cost of building a UI down to under a day, and the cost of changing a UI to hours?"

When you make those changes, you get little apparent progress for the first half of the project and then it all completes so rapidly that the effect of change doesn't have the opportunity to take hold.

The "should cost" and "could cost" analysis may take you away from the one neck theory.

However if you go with "one neck," you should do two things:

- Make sure the portions of the project are loosely coupled so that you could swap out an approach to part of the project without endangering the whole.

- Make sure you are tracking progress and productivity in a way that you could align with your "should cost" or "could cost" analysis, and make changes if it gets out of hand.

The "could cost" for projects of these types are often a few million to tens of millions (it's usually the interfaces and the legacy systems that are the hardest to improve).

If you believe this, as I do, you would realize that you could launch several projects aimed at the "could cost" model, and even if some of them failed, you'd come out far ahead.

However, launching several projects, or even launching one project with several potentially redundant parts, seems wasteful. It is tempting to be "conservative" and take the highest estimate, select the most qualified contractor, put them as the prime contractor, and be content that you have "one neck to choke." In Chapter 7 we introduce an alternative contracting strategy called "leader/follower," which effectively gives you two necks to choke.

FALLACY # 6 "EACH APPLICATION HAS A POSITIVE ROI, THEREFORE MY IT PORTFOLIO MUST BE RETURNING FAR MORE THAN I AM SPENDING"

Most projects these days go through a Return on Investment (ROI) review process. Often these analysis spreadsheets have the precision of evaluating long-term bond options (a great deal of the analysis deals with how much should we discount future savings versus current costs).

However, if you look closely (and I've looked at hundreds of these) you will see one of two things:

- A long list of pretty dubious claims that have been dutifully costed out, and/or

- Some minor benefits that have been costed and a "strategic" reason the project must be done

I'm not opposed to doing systems for strategic reasons. What I'm opposed to is using the strategic reason as an excuse.

Once upon a time back in the 1950's, which is the only time this exchange could feasibly have happened, a husband came home and greeted his wife with "Hi honey, what's for dinner?"

> *"Oh nothing."*
>
> *"Nothing, how come?"*
>
> *"Because the library burned down today."*
>
> *"Oh....Wait a minute, what does the library burning down have to do with our dinner?"*
>
> *"Nothing, really. But when you really don't want to do something, one excuse is as good as another."*

This interaction reminded me of a project one of our clients was involved. It was the replacement of an enterprise-wide Human Resource system. I read the justification statement. There were a few costed benefits such as reassign several legacy programmers and discontinue some license payments, but nothing that would justify the project's $18 million price tag. The benefit that put it over the top was the support for "collective bargaining." Apparently, a big union renegotiation was coming up and the new system was sold on its ability to solve this problem.

Of course, the project ran over budget several-fold (and most of the overrun wasn't even recorded because it got pushed out to user groups' budgets). Nevertheless, this system did eventually go live.

I was talking to one of the survivors of the project a year or so after the conversion, lamenting the overrun. I said, "Well it did run over both budget and schedule, but at least you got the collective bargaining support." The project member just shook his head. "It turned out the project was so late we couldn't wait for it, and we had to implement the collective bargaining features in the old system."

This is a classic example of the library burning down. If the real strategic need was collective bargaining, they would have known ahead of time that that requirement could be satisfied some other way. But because collective bargaining sounded like a good excuse, it could get attached to the solution the promoters of the new system wanted all along.

So my first problem with portfolio theory as applied to systems projects is that the costs are usually "hard costs" (they will get spent and money will leave the organization), and they are usually low by 50-100%. In parallel, the benefits are mostly soft if they are quantified at all (an improvement in productivity of 3% will yield a significant saving). These soft savings only become hard if you do something effective with your 3% productivity improvement, such as layoffs, reassignments, and more throughputs.

It is very rare that anyone ever even attempts to measure the professed benefits after the project is over. It is almost a cliché now for ERP implementation projects to have a disclaimer that most of the benefits will not be realized until more than a year or two after the implementation is complete, which is usually enough time for the consultants to get out of town.

Therefore, we have underestimated hard costs and overestimated soft gains or strategic benefits that are rarely measured. This seems like a problem.

But this isn't the real problem.

The real problem is the externalities. Economists refer to externalities as the cost born by the environment and not born by the perpetrator. When a manufacturer pollutes a river, it has a real cost to the community. Consumers of water may have to spend additionally on purification; sickness incurs additional healthcare costs and the like. Removing the pollutants from the water before returning the water to the river would cost the manufacturer additional money.

In the case of information systems, the externalities often outweigh the benefits the system was meant to deliver. In this case, the externalities include:

- **Increasing the size and complexity of the "data scape."** The data scape is the number of different concepts that much be managed to manage all the data that is being used. Each application that adds another 10,000 attributes to a company's collective set of attributes has increased the complexity and therefore the cost for all the other systems that now must deal with this.

- **Increasing the legacy technical debt burden.** Each additional application system adds more technical debt to the firm. Technical debt is the agile term for unnecessary code complexity that raises the cost of subsequent system changes.

- **Legacy "lock-in."** Every system that gets built increases the opportunity for legacy "lock-in." Legacy lock-in of system A occurs when system B becomes dependent on some aspect of system A. Maybe it's a data feed, an API, or a process to retrieve information from system A. Every incidence of this form of lock-in, makes it harder to dislodge system A, when its time finally comes. Making it more difficult to replace a legacy system is one of the largest drivers of cost in corporations today. This is why the mere implementation of a system increases the externality costs.

One of our prescriptions when proposing a new application is to set up a reclamation budget, and to include in the reclamation budget the total cost of decommissioning the system. The idea of a reclamation budget comes from the regulation of the mining industry, where mining companies are now required to establish and set aside a reclamation budget to restore the environment of a mining project to something resembling what it was before the mine was operated.

So if you survey the wreckage of the systems you have in place and ask yourself: "Where did all these horribly inefficient applications come from?," understand that they are the product of a selection process that rewards "magical thinking" about hard costs and soft benefits, while ignoring the growing costs of piling externality upon externality.

FALLACY # 7 "WE'RE NOT IN THE INFORMATION SYSTEMS BUSINESS"

Many companies use this line to explain why they should not build (or should not even run) their own systems. This line was used to justify a great deal of the outsourcing of information systems.

But is it even remotely true? Once upon a time, when we were mostly an agrarian economy, you could say that most businesses were only marginally in the information business. Even an agrarian society needs some information about relative demand for products and basic information about the inputs needed to optimally grow and harvest their produce, as well as information about weather and markets.

However, ever since we entered the manufacturing age, we became information processing companies. Most processes were initially manual, but eventually most have become automated, to the point that even the smallest café or bed and breakfast relies on information systems to stay in business.

But the question remains. If you are not *primarily* in the systems business (that is, if you do not sell information systems, but merely use them), are you *really* in the information systems business? I would suggest that you very much are.

Even if you do not create software, you use it. The act of using software, especially software that mediates your key processes, puts you in the systems business. If you contemplate changing your business processes, this necessitates changing your information system. If you don't have the ability to change your own software, you are at the mercy of whoever does.

This is one of the lessons that have been learned by companies who have outsourced their information systems. When you outsource your information systems, you have turned over to someone else the exclusive right to change that software and will pay a premium to make changes.

This idea that you pay a premium for changes to outsourced systems arises from the same forces that lead to contractors charging a premium for change orders on projects. First, once a contract or an outsourced arrangement is in place, change orders are the primary source of new revenue for the contractor. Second, changes to complex legacy systems are costly and risky. Most contractors prefer to be conservative when estimating the cost to make a change to ensure that most of the requested changes complete in less than the estimated cost. Third, your outsourcer now has a monopoly on your system change business. Your only real option is to not make a change. However, not changing your system is equivalent to not changing your business, and a business that is not continually evolving is one that is under threat.

We understand why people say they are not in the information systems business. It's mostly because they don't want to be in the information systems business. Additionally, it's often because they were not very good at information system building and information systems implementing. However, *wishing* to leave the systems business is not the same as leaving the systems business.

Think of the small restaurant owner. He or she may not want to be in the advertising business, or the business of recruiting servers, or the business of menu management and pricing, but failing to master any of these is a recipe for failure in the restaurant business.

In the same way, declaring that you are not in the information systems business is a prescription for being in a business that is unable to change gracefully, and ultimately unable to cope.

IDC has come to the same conclusion:

> *Enterprises are turning away from traditional vendors and toward cloud providers. They're increasingly leveraging open source. In short, they're becoming software companies.*[38]

SUMMARY

Stop and think before blindly adhering to clichés. In the chain of software architecture decision and approval, I have encountered many whose thinking is no deeper than these clichés. Unfortunately, these clichés rule our lives instead of real thinking and evaluating of alternatives.

We need to think deeply and critically about software implementation, as these are deep and systemic problems. Relying on clichés in place of thinking is just the opposite.

---

[38] http://bit.ly/2CGxvA3.

CHAPTER 6
The quagmire by sector

This book was gestated in large organizations. However, it will affect many other sectors of the economy.

HOW THE QUAGMIRE LOOKS FOR GOVERNMENT

The government sector is as deep into the quagmire as it gets. We have done more work with state agencies than either local or federal, but our observations of all three suggest that the nonprofit sector is firmly in the quagmire.

Most of the popularized IT runaway projects have come from the public sector. The private sector is better about keeping these things out of the news.

FACTORS MAKING IT WORSE

What is it about the public sector that leads to their over-investment in legacy systems? The following factors conspire to make the situation worse for the government:

- Difficulty in hiring top talent
- Overly restrictive purchasing procedures
- Contractors that specialize in gaming the system
- Willingness to accept mediocracy
- Budget cycles
- Lack of incentive

Difficulty in hiring top talent

Government agencies often lament the fact that their restrictive pay grade systems prevent them from hiring the best and the brightest. There is some truth to this. Add to this the fact that there are no stock options, lavish bonuses, and the like.

For these reasons, hotshot programmers and architects who understand the latest and greatest tools and techniques are less likely to come to the ranks of civil service.

Overly restrictive purchasing procedures

Government agencies pride themselves in their objectivity and freedom from influence by slick marketing types. How this manifests is through very restrictive purchasing procedures. Most government agencies must go through a competitive bid process for all but the most minor procurement. The process itself adds considerable time to any project. There is the process of defining one's requirements in enough detail to write an RFP, which takes months. Then the RFP process itself takes months, because the RFP has to be produced and published, time must be allowed for bidders to respond, followed by an evaluation period, interviews, and time to allow for protests before a project can begin. This can add six months to a project cycle.

If six months are allocated to procurement, there is a strong incentive toward larger projects. Why go out to bid for a one-month project? You will only get two months' worth of work accomplished per year. Better to go with projects longer than a year.

However, this leads right into the larger project/larger failure rate problems.

Contractors that specialize in gaming the system

An entire sub-industry exists due to the size of the government software industry. Pejoratively called "beltway bandits" from their Headquarters near the I-495 beltway around Washington DC, these firms specialize in servicing the government markets.

There is nothing wrong with this per se, but what has happened is these firms have specialized in winning, expanding, and extending government contracts far more than they have specialized in performing them. This is because there is very little incentive in performance, and a great deal of incentive in capture (as they call winning a bid).

Because of the "objective" criteria in the RFPs, and how hard it is to objectively score reputation, the government ends up reinforcing this bad behavior. The beltway bandits know how to answer questions in a way that the contractors are more or less forced to be awarded maximum points. They specialize in protesting when they don't win. Many government employees are fearful of protests, not only because it delays their projects even further, but because it holds them up to scrutiny. We have often worked for government agencies who lament the fact that they "had to" select a contractor that they knew could not perform, because their objective process lead them to a conclusion they knew wouldn't work.

Another popular practice is getting involved with an agency in advance of an RFP and making sure there are requirements that only they can satisfy. This generally favors firms with large marketing firms who can dedicate resources to the long-term cultivation of contacts inside the agency.

Finally, there is the revolving door between agencies and contractors. There are some prohibitions against hiring contractors who employ ex-agency employees, but not nearly enough.

Willingness to accept mediocrity
There is a sort of learned helplessness in many of the agencies we've worked with. This is partially a product of their difficulty in hiring, and partially a result of the contractors learning to prey on them.

This has led to extreme conservatism. If you don't believe you can hire and retain talent, you are unlikely to embark on custom development projects. If you believe that your contractors will game the procurement, you will define projects that have little risk and require little skill.

Budget cycles

Most agencies work in 1-2 year budget cycles. It is very hard to get long-term projects funded.

While this is a disadvantage for long-term improvement projects, in many ways I think it has been more blessing than curse. For many agencies, the 1-2 year cycle has forced it to concentrate on smaller (therefore less risky) projects, and especially to focus on projects that would become operational in far less than a year.

Lack of incentive

The private sector has personal and/or collective incentives that are missing from government and nonprofit sectors. In the private sector, the profit motive trickles down. If you can figure out how a software project can improve productivity or increase revenue, the incentive pay of the affected employees will help make that happen. The head of sales will be happy to get behind a project that will increase revenue, as it will improve commissions for all his salespeople, and an increase in revenue will likely lead to bonuses all around.

Government projects also go through much of the same motions when it comes to justifying projects, such as ROI calculations, featuring improved productivity and improved goal attainment. However, there isn't the same kind of urgency because there aren't personal incentives attached to the initiatives.

FACTORS MAKING IT BETTER

The situation for government agencies need not be as dire as it is. I have painted with broad strokes a general set of problems amongst government agencies, but it needn't always be so. At times government agencies have proven themselves to be motivated, adroit, and taking the right kinds of risks. Consider NASA in the 1960's getting astronauts to the moon and back, or the Department of Transportation and the interstate highway system. We have worked with government agencies who have managed to overcome some of the negative inertia of the above factors and deliver above-average results.

While government agencies have a considerable set of factors to overcome, they have some things going for them that they need to learn to capitalize on. In particular, governments need to learn how to exploit some of the positive factors they have going for them:

- Stability
- Ability to hire pretty good talent
- Longer planning horizons
- Less reliance on packaged software
- Budget cycles

Stability

The stability of government agencies is a strength that isn't leveraged much. Governments rarely go out of business. Businesses routinely do.

Government should be able to capitalize on this more. Many people feel the tug of stability and the potential to work on longer term projects. It is hard to work on long-term projects in firms obsessed with quarterly earnings.

Ability to hire pretty good talent

While government agencies cannot compete for the top talent, they can attract "pretty good talent." We have been privileged to work with people who may not have been "top" but were quite competent. In the long run, having a stable group of competent people may outperform a revolving door of superstars.

Longer planning horizons

Governments are not going away. Their permanence is their strength. They can propose and execute projects that could take a decade or more. When I was with a consulting firm, we would help clients build "Long Range Information Systems Plans." It was rare that we could get clients to pay attention to a three-year plan. I had the fortune of working with two mining companies, which, because of the nature of their business, could think in five year horizons.

Governments routinely think in longer terms—partly because of their permanence, but partly because of their pace. They know things take longer and they plan for it. This is great for making long-term gradual improvements. A small team working over a longer time frame often drastically outperforms a much larger team that attempts to do a project in a compressed timeframe.

Less reliance on packaged software

Even though the government market is large in total, each agency has its own requirements. As such, there isn't a very large reachable market, and therefore there are not as many packaged options available. This may have been a gift in disguise. Many government agencies are less afraid than their private firm counterparts in taking on custom software development projects. When you are comfortable with custom development, you are more likely to change an existing system rather than buy and attempt to integrate another package.

Budget cycles

We mentioned above the negative on budget cycles, but there is a positive. Because of their budgeting cycles, most state and local agencies tend to one or two year projects. There is often no guarantee that a project will continue in the following fiscal year.

The government agencies' response has been to package their projects into less than one-year phases that can be implemented and used even if the next phase isn't funded. Further, because there is a hard stop to the phase, they are generally more conservative in what they put into a phase.

Essentially, they have invented their own form of agile. Longer sprints and epics to be sure, but they still shoot to have an installable product before the end of the budget year. It may not be the "Minimum Viable Product," but it is often a subset of what they would have designed had they had the luxury of doing all their requirements up front.

This is an over generalization. There are agencies that do launch multi-year projects, and there are some that are practicing full agile development. However, I have seen this middle ground so much more often in state and local government that it deserves a mention, and deserves to be encouraged.

GOVERNMENT SUMMARY

Most government agencies are deeply in the application-centric quagmire. Some, especially at the Federal level are deep in the quagmire. As mentioned in the first chapter, some of the attempts to rise up were misinformed, and cost billions of dollars. Our guess is these agencies will have a long memory; it will be a long time until they muster the courage to take another run at it, but it is inevitable.

I'm reminded of a State Teachers' Pension Agency we worked with. They have ancient legacy systems. The Y2K crisis gave them the impetus to take on a massive rewrite of their systems. After $20 million and nothing to show, they cancelled the project. It was almost ten years before the memory of that fiasco died down. We were brought in and designed their new data model and architecture. It was a rather straightforward design; the most complex part was how to engineer an orderly transition from their legacy systems to a properly decoupled Service-Oriented Architecture. We were not in the implementation business at the time. We expect this would be several million dollars and two to three years. We checked in again after three years and they were $34 million into the project with no end in sight. A less formal check in 2017 revealed that the team was still struggling.

One of the main problems with our industry is that there is far more money to be made by being incompetent than there is for being competent.

There are still far too many contractors who make far more money *not* implementing systems than there are contractors that can implement productively. Sadly, it will probably be another ten years before this agency gathers the collective will to take this on again. Ten more years of living with woefully inadequate systems.

THE DEATH AND REBIRTH OF THE APPLICATION SOFTWARE INDUSTRY

There are some interesting signs of life in the application software industry.

The largest packaged application vendors still bulldoze ahead, mostly ushered along by their implementation ecosystem. As Vinnie Mirchandani points out in *SAP Nation*, SAP has had several attempts at remaking its core software but their multi-hundred billion dollar ecosystem brings them back to continued extensions of their flagship product, which is essentially their R/3 product from the 1980's.

However, two trends should worry the large application software vendors. The first is their overreliance on maintenance revenue. Maintenance revenue is the 15-20% of the original purchase price that firms pay for the ongoing privilege of using the software, along with technical support and software feature addition and bug fixes. This is a cash cow for the application software companies. As we have mentioned throughout this book, it is very hard for companies to get off these legacy application systems, even though many are highly motivated to do so.

Somewhere, sometime soon, we will witness "The Last ERP Implementation." Once something is inevitable, it is just a matter of time. We are convinced that the ERP economics are now at least 10 times more expensive than their alternatives and may be 100 times. Inertia will only keep this trend going for so long.

The second area of concern for the traditional application software vendors is their vastly worse economics to their newer nimbler, cloud-based competitors, as well as the existence of open source alternatives. Most of the established application vendors now offer cloud hosting but they haven't changed their licensing or integration economics, so it only affects a small part of the equation. So far, the open source alternatives are not complete enough to be competitive. However, this is the perfect set up for a disruptive innovation. The application software vendors are seeing encroachment at the low end of their markets. They respond to the cloud economics by offering their own cloud versions, without changing their economics.

However, there is hope in the application software market.

The first glimmers are in the App Store and Play, the two marketplaces that Apple and Google have created for Apps on Smart Phones. When Apple launched the App Store, its entire concept was far from mainstream. The software market of 2007, the year of the debut of the iPhone looked like this:

Firm Size	Typical Application Project Size
Large firms	$10 million plus, multi-year projects to implement major applications
Medium business or departmental systems within large firms	$100K - several million dollar implementation projects
Small business	$1,000 plus to implement accounting, CRM and various other systems
Personal	Hundreds of dollars for spreadsheets, office productivity, email and the like

Against this backdrop, Apple chose the price point to be 99 cents, or $1.99 for a premium offering (in addition to a large number of "free" offerings that would make money through ad revenue). One would be excused for considering that this would become a trivial footnote to the evolution of the software industry.

The App Store and Play now represent an $80 billion market.[39] That is 20% of the traditional application software industry. This is a classic disruptor pattern playing out before our eyes. This was made possible through nearly 300 billion downloads.[40] Reflect on this for a second. This is an $80 billion industry, barely 10 years old, whose average sales per item is 25 cents (of the 300 billion downloads many were free).

This industry has created an existence proof. We are beginning to see experiments around how to take this idea to the corporation.

At the moment, the early experiments aren't able to scale to enterprise needs. One example is Zoho, which allows individuals to integrate their many apps together. Another is IFTTT (IF This Then That) which allows people to automate simple tasks. The problem with these apps, is that they rely on individuals owning their systems integration experience, which is something only a small percentage of the population are inclined to do.

---

[39] http://bit.ly/2yRTAIN.

[40] http://bit.ly/2kGxFyY.

The other problem is that while it integrates information for an individual, it does not provide any integration for the firm.

In the companion book, we will take up what the prerequisites are to create this lightweight app experience on top of an integrated enterprise.

Four other related trends are hinting at a way out of the quagmire:

- APIs
- RESTful APIs
- Microservices
- Low code / no code

APIS

Legend has it that Jeff Bezos in 2002 dictated that henceforth all communication between applications would be through well-defined APIs (Application Programming Interfaces).[41] APIs are a predefined way for other applications to access each other's functionality.

APIs have been seen as the solution to the legacy problem. This is certainly a step in the right direction. We don't know all of the details on how it was implemented at Amazon. But we do know it has helped Amazon a great deal. There are other firms that have

---

[41] http://bit.ly/1hCu2EH.

implemented something similar without as good a result. The difference isn't in the use or not of APIs; it is much more in how you do it. Just telling everyone to expose the functionality of their application in an API doesn't solve the problem, because without a lot of discipline, each application will expose their arbitrarily different internal structures and little will have been gained. What is gained is the number of ways to integrate systems has been rationalized, such as by file-to-file transfer and direct database access. ETL has all been eliminated in favor of the API, which is progress.

RESTFUL APIS

Roy Fielding's PhD dissertation[42] reverse-engineered the Web to find the principles that made it successful. One thing he found was something he called "Representational State Transfer" (REST), which included several ideas. One idea is that an API provides a representation of a resource, such as an order might be represented by an HTML page, a pdf document, or a csv file. The second idea which has allowed the web to scale is that state is managed in the client. One very subtle implication of RESTful interfaces is that there are very few verbs with GET, PUT, POST and DELETE being the main ones, yet potentially thousands of nouns for the resources, such as Customers, Orders, and Product.

---

[42] http://bit.ly/2BvRPnH.

A traditional API architecture has lots of compound verbs such as getCustomer, getCustomerOrder, getAddress, updateAddress, and newAddress.

As we will see, the small number of verbs allows architectures to evolve that could better manage network cache and computer memory. If someone had recently issued a GET request for Order27, it would likely still be in computer memory. And the idea that PUTs and POSTs be "idempotent," meaning that executing the same PUT or POST more than once wouldn't change the state of the server, ushered in a set of architectures that no longer had to invest a great deal of infrastructure on guaranteeing that a message got processed only once.

Finally, relying on resources as the nouns greatly reduces the variety that was introduced with traditional APIs.

MICROSERVICES

Microservices is a style of developing enterprise applications that might be characterized as "fine grained SOA" (Service-Oriented Architecture). This is a very promising idea. Microservices are similar to libraries of code, the difference being, with a set of libraries you eventually include and compile the libraries into a monolith. The microservices approach strives to create similar functionality as you might find in a library, but to implement it as a standalone package that can be invoked through a service call. This turns a monolith into something that can be composed, potentially at run time.

Our belief is that a well-designed architecture might be able to recreate all of the behaviors of a legacy application with a few dozen microservices.

LOW CODE / NO CODE

The "low code / no code" movement is picking up steam. What has been true for a decade is now being more widely adopted. There are ways to build complex applications with little or no application code.

Salesforce was one of the early entries into the no code movement. Their contention, which is mostly correct, is that they could build complex applications without application code. This is essentially the "model driven approach." In model driven, the idea is the application is partially or complete derived from a model of the application. In the 1980's and early 1990's, this was code generation. A model of an application could be input to a code generator that would create application code that was derived from the model. This was what the CASE (Computer Aided Software Engineering) tools were. In the early days, the CASE tools created a first version, or a scaffold of the application, upon which a programmer could add.

In the 1990's the technique improved to where complex applications could be generated that did not require programmers to add code, and therefore the application could continue to be maintained by modifying the model.

One breakthrough that is marked by our patent[43] is the ability to build a system where the model is the application; there is no application code, generated or otherwise.

This general idea has resurfaced now as the "low code / no code" movement. We are seeing much more movement in the area of building applications with little or no code (this is in stark contrast to the tens of millions of lines of code that comprise a typical ERP system).

TWO INDUSTRIES UNDER SIEGE

There are two IT sub-industries that are doing very well now, but will be looking more and more like video rental stores in the near future. One is the systems integration business and the other is the legacy modernization business.

They both promote the idea that applications are inherently complex, and therefore it will take a great deal of effort to either integrate or replace them.

SYSTEMS INTEGRATION

The systems integration industry is a bit of a euphemism. At one point, these were consultants called in expressly to "integrate" systems that had been allowed to grow up in a non-integrated fashion. This integration was often

---

[43] http://uspto.org Patent 6,049,673.

opportunistic, even building point-to-point interfaces if that was the most expedient way to solve the problem at hand.

Many of these projects were large. As these firms grew, they needed more and more large projects to feed the backlog.

Most "systems integration" projects now are implementation projects. The firm is implementing new functionality, which co-incidentally also involves a lot of integration.

As described in the first two chapters, many of these projects are 10-100 times more expensive than they need to be, and their success rate hovers in the 50% range, despite decades of methodological attempts to improve it.

As the systems integration business turns into a buyer's market, expect to see the ranks of systems integrators thinned considerably.

LEGACY MODERNIZATION

There are two types of legacy modernization vendors: those that focus on obsolete infrastructure and those that focus on replacing obsolete applications.

If your existing systems are overly dependent on hardware, operating systems, databases, or programming languages that have become obsolete, you could be in the market for the first type of legacy modernization company.

If you have a major application that was coded in languages such as PowerBuilder, Natural, or DataBasic, it may behoove you to do a straight port to something that you can find programmers to work on.

Most of these vendors focus on a particular legacy platform. The key to success in these projects is to avoid the temptation to make functional changes to the system while the conversion is in progress. You will want as pure a "lift and convert" as is possible. You can make the functional changes in the new environment after the conversion settles down.

You should consider conversions like this to be tactical. Direct translation of your legacy code from one language to another will not magically make it more malleable. Nor will lifting a schema from one database and dropping it on another make it more than a little bit more flexible. However, it may buy you some time.

The other legacy modernization vendors concentrate on replacing your existing applications with more modern ones.

As we will discuss later in this chapter, what makes the lift and replace strategy so much harder than it seems, is that the existing systems do not have the same boundaries as the system being installed. We have this convenient fiction that an ERP system is an ERP system, but the truth is that every install has a wildly different footprint and has different sets of dependencies each of which has to be addressed.

The real problem is that most "new applications" have most of the same economic issues as the systems they are replacing. Indeed, many have the problem in an even more severe fashion. Most are far more complex and are harder to change than the systems they are replacing.

OUTSOURCING

The pendulum tends to swing both ways on these industries. Ever since H. Ross Perot invented outsourcing at EDS, firms have been alternately drawn to it, and often wished they hadn't been.

Some of the early outsourcing was financially motivated. A firm, strapped for cash, could get an infusion from an outsourcing firm, which bought their IT assets in exchange for a long-term contract. The outsourcers aim, often achieved, was to make more over the years of the contract than the upfront investment. They could often do this even while reducing the cost per transaction, at least in part by employing ever-cheaper hardware and networks. Generally speaking, outsourcers were not motivated to reduce the cost of change, and were certainly not incentivized to make major architectural improvements. They merely sought to reduce the cost of change, as change orders were large and lucrative line items.

Conversely, the outsourcing arrangements that seem to have worked out best for clients were those in areas where there was little need for change and customization. Furthermore, there was a low switching cost, which allowed the client to continually shop the outsource arrangement. The traditional 100% outsourcing of an IT shop typically does not allow any part of the system to be switched out. This is especially problematic if the outsource contract locks in long-term rates that become unfavorable.

Email is pretty much a commodity now. Firms can outsource their email, without having major side effects on other systems. It is relatively easy to shop email, and switch when it becomes advantageous. Email is a stable stand-alone application. Over time email will become a feature in many systems, and firms will be looking for better ways to integrate their many communication channels. At that point, email may no longer be a good outsource candidate, but for now it is an exemplar.

Outsourcing parts of the stack will continue to create favorable economics. Cloud computing is outsourcing your hardware and operating system infrastructure. The internet is outsourcing your computer network.

On the other extreme, non-commodity, highly customized systems, such as ERP systems, are not very good candidates for outsourcing. The outsourcing arrangement tends to lock in the inefficient cost structure.

Our prediction is that outsourcing will continue to grow for the commoditized portions of the solution, and will gradually begin to shrink for the custom and changeable parts of the application infrastructure.

OFFSHORING

The offshoring industry is essentially moving work to places where labor is cheaper. In this regard, it is much like the offshoring of manufacturing or garment production. At one level, it is easier, as we can sling code around the world at the speed of light, where fabric and plastic still move at the speed of container vessels.

The other relevant aspect of offshoring software is that the technology is constantly changing, as are the requirements.

Each wave of offshoring boosts local demand for the skill being offshored.

Garment manufacturers originally moved production to China. As wages in the garment industry rose, many moved their operations to India. Even with their vast reserves of labor, wages began going up in China and India. Garment makers moved to Vietnam and

Bangladesh[44] as well as Indonesia, Malaysia, Sri Lanka, the Philippines, and Korea.[45]

So far, software outsourcers haven't followed this pattern. This is at least in part due to language barriers, and the relatively low level of technical college training in the lower-wage countries. Software outsourcers have tended to go where talent is high, and the costs (while not at the Bangladesh garment level) are still competitive. These are countries like Bulgaria, Hungary, Lithuania, and Portugal.

Much of the offshoring business, indeed most programming, will become partially or completely automated in the coming decades, and dry up the demand for offshore technologists.

For the medium term, there is still an advantage in offshoring legacy maintenance, and some systems integration, but more and more firms will understand this to be a rear-guard action.

The other area that will prosper in the medium term will be advanced technology. Many pockets of expertise will spring up around technologies like machine learning, natural language processing and big data.

---

[44] http://cnnmon.ie/2jbV2A4.

[45] http://bit.ly/2oDImb4.

THE NEW PLATFORM VENDORS

What are already emerging are new categories of platform vendors. There is a great attraction in being a platform vendor.

A platform vendor is someone who creates the infrastructure in which a whole ecosystem is based. The most valuable platforms are the "two-sided" platforms.

For instance, Amazon is a two-sided platform. It is a sales platform to buyers of consumer goods, but in the early days when it was only selling its own merchandise, it was a one-sided platform. Once it opened its platform up to vendors and allowed them to sell their own merchandise, it became a two-sided platform.

These two-sided platforms have incredible network effects. Once you have the majority of the online buyers, it is easier to attract additional sellers. Adding additional sellers just increases the demand on the buyer side.

While Amazon is a platform for physical goods, there are many purely digital platforms. Apple's App Store (and its predecessor iTunes) and Google's Play are application platforms. And Amazon's AWS business is a platform for cloud offerings.

Salesforce started life as a SaaS (Software as a Service) provider, but once it opened up its development capability it too became a two-sided platform, and currently most of its revenue comes from applications they did not develop.

There are tools now that will allow for DIY (Do It Yourself) integration such as Zoho and IFTTT, but these may not scale well. There will evolve a few platforms, and eventually one dominant platform, that will flip the current application-centric paradigm on its head, and these will scale well.

HOW APPLICATION CENTRICITY ROBS PRODUCTIVITY FROM SMALL BUSINESS

Small business might be the segment of the economy least affected by the quagmire.

The very small business (1-10 employees) typically has an accounting system (QuickBooks more often than not) and a series of other task-specific applications, depending on what they do. They will often have SaaS (Software as a Service) applications for things like CRM (Customer Relationship Management) or Inventory Management. They will often have their email list managed by someone like Constant Contact or Mail Chimp.

If you look closely, you will notice that they have data integration issues. For example, the customers in the CRM system have to be re-entered into their accounting system in order to be invoiced. Some of their contacts are redundant between their CRM system and their email management system.

But the problem is more of a nuisance than a strategic barrier. It can mostly be handled with some redundant data entry, and if they miss a few, it's not that big a deal.

Eventually, when the new platform vendors, described in the previous section, hit their stride, we expect the small business point solutions, whether on premise or cloud-based, will be under threat, but until then, this is the sector least affected.

As small firms get bigger, their applications systems tend to become more numerous and more complex. My peers in the CEO group called Vistage used to refer to our business as "cleaning up hairballs." They said that growing small businesses need a "hairball prevention service." They bought into the idea that there were things they were unwittingly doing that would eventually lead to issues that would require a great deal of effort to unwind, and that paying attention and preventing this could be worth a fair bit.

A growing body of research suggests that they were on to something. In the study of small business growth, several authors have identified "crises" that must be navigated for a small company to emerge and grow to become a large company[46] especially Larry Greiner's work on how companies grow through five predictable crises.[47]

---

[46] http://bit.ly/1J5A1PR.

[47] http://bit.ly/1DvsB4V.

The last crisis in Greiner's original work was described as the crisis of red tape followed by the collaboration growth phase. This last phase has been reinterpreted as the integration phase, as most small companies got to this point building out silos as fast as they could.

SUMMARY

The quagmire is playing out quite differently in different sectors. The public sector arguably has more legacy software per capita than any other sector. It has a few things going for it, such as an embrace of agile and lean, but far more working against it, including difficulty hiring the talent needed to get them out of the quagmire, and an industry (the "beltway bandits") that is dedicated to keeping them in the quagmire.

The application software and the system integration industries may be the most threatened. In the end game, they are slated to go from about $400 billion per year for each of the two industries, to asymptotically close to $0 billion. This won't happen overnight but it will be even more extreme than the change for the public sector, as the public sector will at least still exist, even though it will take them quite a while to crawl out of the wreckage of their legacy systems.

Small business and the digital native companies (those founded after 2000) will fare the best, as they have invested the least in the quagmire.

CHAPTER 7
Turning the tide

What can you do now to begin to get out of the quagmire?

ASSESSMENT

The first thing is to take stock. Determine if you are in the quagmire. In order to take action you likely need to take an inventory, and get some metrics.

This section is about getting a handle of how bad the problem is in your organization.

INVENTORY OF APPS

The first step is to get a simple count of the number of applications you are currently supporting. With each application get two statistics:

- **Schema size.** Number of tables plus total number of columns for relational systems, number of classes plus total number of attributes for object-oriented systems, number of terminal elements plus total number of attributes for XML-based systems, etc.

- **Number of lines of code.** The number you have access to and are maintaining, and don't count code you can't modify.

This will give you the factors you need to assess the total complexity of your information infrastructure.

FUNCTIONALITY MAP

Construct a functional decomposition of the key business functions your organization performs. Keep this at a high level, for example, record resource consumption, establish, or record obligations, record assets transfers including cash, record physical movement, and record production. Create a companion list of facets that qualify these basic functions, such as the type of product being produced, type of materials whose movements are being tracked, or the geographical or organizational sub divisions that might form boundaries for application systems.

Then categorize each application by the functions and the qualifying facets. This should begin to suggest opportunities for rationalization. However, wait until you complete the dependency exercise to determine the sequence of execution.

INTERFACES

Very few companies have a good inventory of the interfaces they have in place, which are costing money to support and that are hampering their attempts to migrate systems. There are several approaches to this step, depending on the number and complexity of your interfaces.

If you have less than a couple of hundred applications, you may find it easier to visually map the known interfaces and invite maintenance programmers to opine on the missing interfaces. It is best to get many of them in the room at the same time, as they tend to riff on one another and "remember" interfaces that they may otherwise have forgotten.

At more than a few hundred apps, you will need some automated support. Several software firms can help with this, including Eccenca, GlobalIDs, and Io-Tahoe. After you have profiled your data and determined that six different systems have identical histograms for certain datasets such as customer or product lists, the next step is to instrument the systems in real time and figure out which one is getting populated first and by implication, which ones have interfaces and are being fed.

You also need to map all the dependencies between your applications and operating systems, databases, network protocols, and computer hardware.

You want to map the dependency at the level it exists. If an application is dependent on a particular version of a database or an operating system, you need to document that.

If possible, document these dependencies graphically. If not, document them in a graph database and draw various subsets. What you are most interested in are deep chains of dependencies, and areas where only a few applications depend on a technology, as that may be an easier technology to "sunset."

MAP YOUR DEPENDENCIES

Three things make getting rid of legacy systems harder than it should be:

- The functional boundaries are arbitrary
- There are many deep dependencies that have accreted over time
- They are mostly a black box

In this section, we'll cover some tips for the first two, and the following section is about the last bullet.

At a first order of approximation, applications line up with business functions. Never mind the fact that there isn't anywhere a good list of business functions, as every time we have looked at a client we see combinations of extremely generic functions, with business processes and categories.

Reflecting on this for just a moment or two, we realize this alignment just doesn't exist. Take the function "Accounts Receivable." Most companies have this functionality in dozens of their systems, and this functionality doesn't have a crisp boundary. In some cases, it involves creation of the invoice. In other areas, it includes collection. Some have customer master file maintenance, many have cash application, and some assess fees and penalties. Most include aging and reporting.

Even more difficult for planning the replacement is figuring out the scope of each application. Sometimes the scope is geographic (this is AR for North America), for some the scope will be customer type (customer segments), and for others the scope is product or service type (separate AR functionality for claims over payment, elevator permits, or audit result fees and penalties).

Generally speaking, you are going to need to replace narrow point solutions with broader flexible solutions. For example, you can replace the AR for North American elevator permits with a general AR solution more easily than you will replace broad AR with a North American elevator permit system. At a minimum, this still requires two things: understanding where the functionality is and what functions the general solution must support.

First thing to do is catalog all your applications and cross-reference them to their scope. Unfortunately, this can be a fair bit of work, but it is essential. Create an inventory of applications, as a matrix to the various facets that define their scope (business function, geography, entity type, and internal organization). This will be the key resource for planning.

The next step is to create from this a dependency map. Each row on the matrix will become a node in a graph. If you have fewer than 150 applications, you may be able to draw this directly, otherwise you'll have to rely on some graph visualization tool. You need to document all the dependencies. The most common are:

- Database (vendor and version)
- Middleware technology
- Programming languages
- Inter-application dependencies (an application will be dependent on other applications that feed it data)
- Third party data feeds
- APIs

These dependencies are mostly one-way (thankfully). An application will depend on a database, but I don't know of any cases where a database depends on an application.

This resource is going to tell you how to proceed. You may want to weaken dependencies, for instance. If you find that an application is dependent on APIs in a particular version of an operating system, you may want to scan the code (see the next section) and profile the API calls. Often, a small number of APIs lock you into a particular version dependency. You can generally make changes to the code to replace those calls with those that depend on more stable parts of the API. While there is still a dependency, it has moved from a particular version of the operating system to a particular brand of operating system. This may not sound like a lot, but it's surprising the flexibility some small shifts like this can improve.

We have contemplated, but never implemented, the idea of metrics of dependency, which would be helpful in a long-term legacy improvement project.

It will help to get a total picture of the internal and external costs to support the applications and their supporting infrastructure. If you can break it down by application or group all the better, but even if you can't this will provide metrics to justify what needs to be done.

STARTING TO EXTRICATE YOURSELF

Recognizing where we are doubling down on bad investments is the beginning of turning this around. We believe that the end game, a world where application implementation will cost a fraction of what it does now, and where system conversions are a thing of the past, will require embracing the Data Centric Revolution, as covered in the companion book. In the meantime, there are many things you can do to free up wasted resources, and prepare for your future:

- Stop the bleeding
- Set up metrics for cost of change and complexity
- Adopt leader/follower practice
- Bake off
- True contingency
- Reverse engineer your legacy systems
- Launch pilots where you need skills
- Build an enterprise ontology

STOP THE BLEEDING

We work with state agencies a fair bit. Recently one agency retained some consultants who convinced them of two things that we happen to agree with, but we were amazed they got agreement on. The two things were:

- The several projects underway were unlikely to end well and were not going to progress the agency toward their desire of getting off their legacy systems, and
- The money freed up by cancelling these projects would immediately fund some more broadly scoped initiatives that were much more likely to help them toward their goal of getting off their legacy systems.

This is very impressive. It is easy to get caught in the year-to-year application replacement cycle, but as we've discussed throughout this book, most of these projects, while they have some tactical advantages often result in strategic backsliding.

This is a largely transferrable strategy, but a bit gutsy to execute. There are usually only two times when this can be executed: when new leadership takes over, or when consultants are brought in at a very strategic level.

In most organizations, it is very hard to get substantial funding for initiatives that address the systemic issues because they don't have immediate payoff. At the same time, there is usually more than enough budget in tactical projects that are approved or underway. This also has the advantage of not having to wait through another budget cycle.

This particular agency is off to a great start. Of course that is no assurance that they will succeed in this endeavor, but they are certainly on the right track, and continuing would have only deepened their technical and integration debt.

SET UP METRICS FOR COST OF CHANGE AND COMPLEXITY

It borders on being a cliché, but it is so true and powerful, I'm going to repeat it: "you can't manage what you don't measure."

What a good metrics program does is focus everyone's attention on the same (and hopefully correct) measures. Many metrics programs suffer from measuring that which is easy to measure. We already mentioned some of the worst things you can measure, such as "lines of code / developer day." Even metrics that most would agree seem reasonable, like schedule and budget attainment, can backfire if they are the only or primary measures. They tend to encourage overly conservative estimating and have project managers emphasize cost over delivering benefits.

Good metrics programs have a few, very important metrics, even if they are not the easiest metrics to gather.

What we want to encourage are metrics that measure the overall health of the information infrastructure, such that a project that makes things worse overall would have a high hurdle to overcome.

A good metrics program would give an overall measure of "goodness" (Are we getting better over time?) but would also be able to single out existing systems and help understand which ones are contributing the most to the dis-economy.

Two metrics that have the most promise (but these are not easy to measure) are:

- Overall complexity
- Cost of change

Overall complexity
This is a measure that you can start simply, and then crank it up as your data gathering improves. The first order approximation of complexity is the total number of

concepts under management. Concepts are classes (e.g. tables, entities) and properties (e.g. columns, attributes, elements). You may want to count enumerated values (e.g. drop-down lists) but only if they are called out in programs or queries. In a traditional system, almost all the classes and properties contribute to the overall complexity of the code that manages it. What the enumerated values do is a system-by-system call. Some systems or styles of development encourage people to code against the controlled vocabulary, which means they contribute to the complexity.

This measure can be gathered by system. You will quickly find out which applications are contributing the most to the overall complexity of your info-scape. You might think that your larger or more complex applications are entitled to add the most to the overall complexity, but this isn't always the case. Some systems are just arbitrarily complex.

If you decommission a complex system, you should take credit for it. By the way, many systems project start off with the intention of decommissioning a system, but end up co-existing with it. This is pretty much the worst of all worlds, as the old complexity persists and the new adds to it.

Cost of change

This one is hard to measure in a way that is comparable across systems, but it is the most important. In a well-designed agile environment, the cost of making a single incremental change is low. In most legacy environments the cost of making a similar change is very high.

What we need is visibility into the gradient between these two extremes, which is where most applications live. The easier thing that many firms have is a log of change requests and changes implemented. The famous "legacy backlog" is the long list of change requests that haven't yet been implemented because they are hard. Most firms do not have access to the "shadow backlog" which are changes that users would like but don't even bother to submit because they would take so long to implement.

By the way, the presence of a rogue system such as one developed in Microsoft Access or Excel, might be a good proxy for change metrics. No one wants to build a rogue system. People build rogue systems because they have a need that would be too hard to implement in the existing systems. About half of the rogue systems we have examined are systems where someone wants to view existing data using a category that doesn't exist in the base data, and then do some simple calculations. Keep in mind that if the cost of change was low, there would be no need for rogue systems.

At the first level of approximation, it would be good to get an idea of the overall cost of change by application. How much are we spending on maintenance for this system?

At the second level, we must figure out how deep the change backlog is and if possible, estimate the shadow backlog or rogue systems that have been spawned. A powerful metric is the comparable change cost of one system over another.

A good cost-of-change system would help an analyst predict the cost of the change by understanding the complexity of the environment. The very statistics that help an analyst predict the cost of change will rapidly shine a light on the issues.

ADOPT LEADER/FOLLOWER PRACTICE

The defense industry has a practice which they occasionally follow, called the "leader/follower." The goal is to avoid becoming overly dependent on a single defense contractor.

The essence of the idea is to award a major weapons program primarily to the winner of the RFP, but to award a portion of it to one of the rivals. You may decide that Contractor A will get 80% of the orders for a new fighter jet or intercontinental ballistic missile. Contractor B will get the other 20%. Contractor B is at an economy of scale disadvantage. However, what may make up for their disadvantage are the incentives. After two years, the customer reevaluates performance of A and B. If B is outperforming A, B gets the 80% for the next two years and A must take the 20%. This is the strategy NASA is using for the Space Station resupply contract. Boeing has been awarded the leader contract at $4.2 billion and SpaceX the follower contract at $2.6 billion.[48]

In the absence of the leader/follower arrangement, "A" (who has 100% of the contract) is motivated to issue change orders and claim that the work is "way harder than it seemed." Moreover, the customer is more or less stuck with accepting this.

In the leader/follower model, this is a prescription to have your book of business cut by 75%.

Conversely, the follower is incented to invest in anticipation of a fourfold increase in revenue. This is a brilliant way to flip becoming captive to your vendor to reinstating market-based competition, even if it is only a market of two.

To make this work in software, there is a need to make sure the assignable work is interchangeable. This entails that there are no proprietary dependencies, and that the specifications are transparent and easily ported. While this takes a bit of discipline, it's hard to imagine any effort with a higher payoff.

BAKE OFF

Instead of launching a $100 million implementation project (and therefore being limited to the small pool of companies who have "successfully" implemented $100

---

[48] http://bit.ly/2C4AqT0.

million projects in your particular subdomain), consider a bake off or a tournament.

Most companies would be far better off instead of launching a $100 million project, to award 10 companies $1 million each to build a MVP (Minimum Viable Product) version of the system.

You will have invested $10 million. You will have at least three viable solutions (10% of the way into a $100 million project to have a 50% chance that you are 10% of the way toward a solution).

Double down with three of the best from the bake off, give them each $2 million more to enhance or elaborate their solution. Add in some requirements you had not previously shared, to judge how well each solution accommodates unanticipated change. Now you are out $16 million. Not only will you have at least one solution that will work, you will know the cost of change. Any additional requirements that haven't been articulated can easily be estimated. Compare this to the traditional approach: all unanticipated changes are change orders, and very expensive ones at that.

At this point, it should be easy to pick a winner, and invest whatever $5 million or $10 million to finish the requirements, conversion, and rollout. The risk is virtually eliminated. The cost is 10-20% of what it would have been.

TRUE CONTINGENCY

Almost all large software projects have a contingency budget. Typically, this is 10-20% of the total project budget. The estimator will tell you there is a 90% likelihood that the actual project cost will fall within this range.

If you study the history of large software projects, you'll agree that this is ridiculous. Large software projects do not distribute around a mean with one or two standard deviations being +/- 10 or 20%. (By the way, no software project ever comes in under budget. *Ever*.)

Steve McConnell invented a test to help people understand how well they can estimate confidence intervals. Go ahead and take the test before you read on:

> *https://blog.codinghorror.com/how-good-an-estimator-are-you/*

We don't want to give away the result, but most estimators are overly confident in the accuracy of their estimates.

Suffice it to say, the contingency for a software implementation project is far too low. In addition, the implementer knows it is too low. They will charge up to the contingency before they get into the charge order business.

However, you have another option: spend your contingency budget on a contingency.

Here is how this would work:

- Let's say you have a $100 million project, and therefore a $20 million contingency.

- You take some percentage of that contingency (say 20% of the 20%, or 4% of the original budget) and launch a "contingency project."

- Best to have a bit of stealth around this, we suggest calling the contingency project a "fully functioning prototype."

- The purported aim of the "fully functioning prototype" is to allow you to work out a lot of UX (user experience) and data quality issues. You can try out different user interfaces and see what will work long before committing to a particular strategy. Likewise, you can get a lot of lead time on your data quality issues.

- But the real point of it being "fully functional" is that you will have a version of the system working with full data volumes, ready to step in should the main contractor get in trouble, and thereby need the contingency.

- You also inform the prime contractor that you have spent the contingency, and that it is not available to them. You needn't tell them what you are doing. They either wouldn't believe you or would try to sabotage it.

In the worst case, you will have spent 4% of your project budget on a "second opinion" and on a working laboratory for the user experience. In the best case, you implement the fully functioning prototype.

REVERSE ENGINEER YOUR LEGACY SYSTEMS

One of the things that keep legacy systems in place is the fear of the unknown. Employees know that the system works–they know there is a great deal of cumulative wisdom and response to previous requirements captured in the legacy system. But rarely does anyone feel confident enough to replace them, due to uncertainty about the adverse effects of abandoning the legacy system.

The truth is most legacy systems have found very complex ways to do very simple tasks. People believe there are complex business rules and algorithms hidden in the vastness of their codebases. There is a bit of truth to this, and in most of the cases where we have looked the real functionality is marbled throughout long stretches of code (one bit of code will set an indicator, another will pick up on the indicator and do some calculation, another will pick up the calculation and use it to categorize a customer or a vendor). All this is just classification. Most classifications can be done in a single step. When you put the logic in one place, it is easy to change it or eliminate it when it no longer serves it purpose. When you spread it around, no one feels confident enough to eliminate a step, because nobody knows what the downstream effect might be.

To counter this paralyzing conservatism, you need comprehensive data. The two best sources are the application code and the persisted data.

Code understanding systems

Systems that parse source code and reverse engineer its meaning have gotten better and better. At a first level of approximation, they can whittle down huge amounts of code to manageable subsets. The ground truth is that most of the code in a legacy application is doing little more than moving data back and forth. The data is moved from the database to some intermediate representation such as copybooks in the COBOL days, object structures in the Java and C++ days, and dictionaries and arrays in JavaScript, Python, and their cousins. It is moved again to APIs, transactions, or representations on the screen. There are tiny bits of logic amid all this moving, such as if the amount field is negative, move it to the credit attribute, otherwise move it to the debit attribute.

Anyone familiar with mining may have heard the term "overburden." This refers to the dirt that must be scraped away before you can reach the valuable ore. Most of the code in enterprise systems is the equivalent of overburden. Scraping it away makes looking for the nuggets easier.

The second level of low-grade functionality is validation, constraint, and integrity management. This is often the second largest category of code in a legacy system, and is often sprinkled throughout. Valid values for enumerations are often in code, as are routines to check for the presence of keys in other tables. When you recognize these patterns, you have another major category of code that you can easily describe and not fear.

Understanding legacy code will also help you find dead code. There is a lot of code in your existing system that is unreachable. Maybe it was code in packaged software that can't be reached because of the way you configured it. Maybe code was prepared to handle conditions that can no longer be set.

Some legacy-understanding software can monitor systems and can report on code that cannot be reached, as well as code that wasn't reached over a long period. This isn't as convincing as a static analysis that can prove that code isn't reachable, but it is a strong indicator that if over time a chunk of code hasn't been accessed, conditions in the business may have changed such that this code isn't needed.

The goal of this exercise is to whittle down a large system to the small amount of code that actually contains important business logic. It is often surprising how little truly algorithmic code exists, and how easily it can be replicated in modern environments. When you strip away most of the repetitive and redundant code, there is often little left. A complex inventory system might have a few algorithms buried in it to set reorder points, calculate efficient order sizes, and flag unusual demand patterns. This is augmented by some very simple logic around re-determining average item cost based on recent receipts and choice of costing method.

I once managed the building of a very complex custom ERP system for a continuous processing manufacturing company making lot-based materials with highly overlapping specifications. The system managed four forms of outbound logistics: a rail car fleet, trucks, containerized shipping, and air shipments. It also contained complex contracts, complex sales incentive compensations, and an ISO-certified laboratory management system. We built this system using a model driven approach that generated code based on simple descriptions of base functionality. In the end, less than 2% of the 3 million lines of code in the system were custom written. This was a much more complex system than most of the systems we see in place in most companies. Once decomposed, it is not uncommon for less than 1% of an application systems code to be responsible for all the custom functionality.

One other thing you want your legacy code-understanding project to do is find and document the dependencies that are baked into your code. This will update the dependency analysis we mentioned earlier and give you a view that will tell you what things will break when you change out various components.

One bit of good news here. By tying the dependencies to licensing costs, it is often possible to pay for the legacy modernization project in its early phases by some strategic rationalization of licensed components in the infrastructure.

Data understanding

A benefit of understanding the legacy system is understanding the data in this system. Again, many tools will help with this endeavor.

First create an automated profile of the data in your existing systems. This will tell you if the metadata defined isn't doing anything and the data you have provides no information.

If you have a table with 20 columns, and only half of them are populated, there is a reasonable chance that you have code in your legacy systems that is "moving" data from the cells these empty columns represent to attributes which will also be empty. If the code is not moving the empty data, it is often testing for nulls, which is still superfluous work.

The next case is a data value that never varies. We often see tables with values that are the same for every row. This usually isn't a coincidence. There is a configuration in the system that has set this value as a constant and repeated it in every row. This happens when implementing a package. Application software vendors often build flexibility into their packages and then constrain it at implementation time. For instance, there may be the potential to have multiple currencies in a purchasing system. If the configuration says that the currency will always be in US dollars, this field gives no new information. The data would be as rich without repeating that at every row.

This is the low hanging fruit, but just harvesting the low hanging fruit will simplify a model considerably. Many products take the analysis to the next level, where they generate histograms for all the values encountered in a given column. The pattern and value set tells a lot. First, it will spot the foreign key / primary key relationships, even if they aren't being managed by the database management system. This is even more powerful across applications.

A data understanding product will detect a set of values in a system. We know them as customer ids, but the data understanding system only knows them as a histogram of values. When it detects the exact same histogram in another system, it rightfully concludes that these two columns represent the same thing.

Some of the more sophisticated data understanding systems look into the metadata or into patterns in related data to find some initial semantic distinctions. When it finds a column that is exclusively filled with numbers that match the United States social security pattern, it makes two initial assessments: this column represents social security number identifiers, and that the row represents people. If it has deduced a histogram for a person id, and finds that same histogram in another table or even another system, then it concludes that the other column is also referring to the same set of people.

This type of analysis can often reduce the complexity of the data scape by a factor of 10 or more.

Legacy understanding

Understanding your legacy system is a lot of work, but the alternative is far direr. We have watched ill-conceived legacy modernization programs invest hundreds of millions of dollars only to flounder when the implementers could not assure sponsors that the replacement system would not overlook some important use cases that the current system handles well.

Once you understand the dependencies, have uncovered the small part of your data model that is in play, and documented the rules in the application code that will need to be brought forward, you will have taken most of the risk out of your legacy modernization program.

There is still a lot of work to do, but when you shine a light on all the risks before you start, you may proceed with confidence.

LAUNCH PILOTS WHERE YOU NEED SKILLS

You will be replacing your legacy systems with something. Your main choices are a "neo legacy" system. That is, a system with all the economic characteristics of a legacy system, but done with modern languages, or a modern system.

Your developers will want to implement a neo legacy system. They won't say it in those terms but they do. They don't want to change the way they think, they just want to learn some new more marketable skills.

Being aware of this you can layer in some trendy technology with the long-term change you're trying to establish. You will also need to establish multi-disciplinary teams. You will want to define projects that will build individual skills as well as corporate competence.

Corporate competence in this area comes from being open and sharing. For instance, you might stand up a RESTful endpoint to allow internal users to access your reference data. Each group that uses this learns several things simultaneously:

- They learn that effort can be saved by sharing

- They learn how to consume a RESTful endpoint

- If you make the code available internally they can learn how it was built, and could do something similar for their subdomain

- It may cause other reference data sets to come out of the woodwork

The multi-disciplinary teams that you sponsor should contain roles for:

- Modern development languages

- Semantic modeling, which is an important skill in economizing and rationalizing data models

- Agile scrum masters to promote and implement agile principles

- Specific technology areas, such as:
  - Natural Language Processing
  - Social Media Data Processing
  - Predictive Analytics
  - Machine Learning
  - Data Science
  - Big Data and Spark
  - Statistical Languages such as R or NumPy
  - Web Scraping
  - Graph Based Visualization
  - Model Driven Development
  - Data Profiling
  - Containerization
  - Semantic Technology

BUILD AN ENTERPRISE ONTOLOGY

An enterprise ontology is like an enterprise data model, but is typically 100 times simpler, and is far more flexible.

Your enterprise ontology will form a simple stable core for all your additional endeavors.

A core model is an elegant, high fidelity, computable, conceptual and physical data model for your enterprise.

Let's break that down a bit.

Elegant

By elegant we mean appropriately simple, but not so simple as to impair usefulness. All enterprise applications have data models. Many of them are documented and up to date. Data models come with packaged software, and often these models are either intentionally or unintentionally hidden from the data consumer. Even hidden though, their presence is felt through the myriad screens and reports they create. These models are the antithesis of elegant. We routinely see data models with thousands of tables and tens of thousands of columns, to solve simple problems. Most large enterprises have hundreds to thousands of these data models.

Our experience tells us that at the heart of most large enterprises lies a core model that consists of fewer than 500 concepts, qualified by a few thousand taxonomic modifiers. When we use the term "concept" here, we mean a class (set, entity, or table) or property (attribute, column, or element). An elegant core model is typically 10 times simpler than the application it is modeling, 100 times simpler than a sub domain of an enterprise, and at least 1000 times simpler than the "datascape" of a large firm.

High fidelity

An overly simple model is not terribly useful. Sure, we could build a model that says that customers place orders for products. This is literally true, but not sufficiently detailed to build systems to drive analytics. This is the main reason that application data models have gotten complex: an attempt to represent requisite detail.

But virtually every application we've looked at has way overshot the mark, and done it poorly to boot. When they encounter a new requirement, application developers tend to do one of two things: write some code to address it, or amend the data model to address it (and then write some more code). It rarely occurs to them to consider a way to represent the distinction that would be reusable. Furthermore, very often the additions being made to a model are "distinctions without a difference." That is, they add something that was "required" but never used in a way that affected any outcome.

Our lens for fidelity is this: if the distinction is needed to support "data structuration," business rules, or classification for retrieval or analytics, then you need that distinction in the model. I have grown very fond of the phrase "data structuration," which is one of the terms that our European customers use. It essentially means decisions around how you want your data structured. So if you decide that you need to store different information on exempt employees versus non-exempt employees, then you need to be able to represent that distinction in the model.

For business rules, if you charge more to insure convertibles than hard top cars, then the model has to have a place to keep the distinction between the two. If your users want to sort their customer lists between VIPs and riff raff, then the model needs that distinction. If your analytics need to aggregate and do regressions on systolic versus diastolic blood pressure readings, then you must keep that distinction.

You'd be forgiven for believing this justifies the amount of complexity found in most data models. It doesn't. For the most part these necessary distinctions are redundantly (but differently) stored in different systems, and distinctions that could easily be derived are modeled as if they could not be.

The real trick we have found is determining which distinctions warrant being modeled as concepts (classes or properties) and which can be adequately modeled as taxonomic distinctions. The former have complex relationships between them. Changing them can disrupt any systems depending on them. The later are little more than tags in a controlled vocabulary, which are easier to govern and evolve in place.

The other trick for incorporating the needed distinctions is the judicious use of faceting. Taxonomists today feel the urge to create a single rooted, giant taxonomic tree to represent their domain. There are generally many smaller, orthogonal facets trapped in those big trees. Extricating them will not only reduce the overall complexity, it has the added benefit of making the pieces far more reusable than the whole.

We have found the secret to high fidelity coupled with elegance is in moving as many distinctions as possible to small, faceted taxonomies. Facets are small, independent ways to categorize things.

Computable

A computable model is one that a program can do something useful with directly.

By analogy, it is the difference between a paper Rand McNally road map and Google Maps. Both model the same territory. Either one might be more or less useful for the purpose at hand. Either could be more detailed. However, the Google Map is computable in a way the paper map isn't. You can ask Google Maps for a route between two points. You can ask Rand McNally all day long, but nothing will happen. You can ask Google what coffee shops are nearby.

A data model on a whiteboard is not computable, nor is one in Visio. Sophisticated data modeling tools give some computability, but this is often not available in the final product. Rand McNally probably uses Geospatial Information System software to build their maps, but it is no longer present in the delivered environment.

The core model that we advocate continues to be present, in its original design form, in the delivered application. It can be interrogated in ways previously only available in the design environment.

Conceptual and physical

Received wisdom these days is that a data model is a conceptual model, a logical model, or a physical model. This is mostly driven from the construction analogy where a conceptual model is the architect's drawings, the logical models are the blueprints, and the physical model is the item actually built.

In the data world, these models are often derived from each other. More specifically, the logical is derived from the conceptual and the physical from the logical. Sometimes these derivations are partially automated. To the extent the transformation is automated, there is more likely to be some cross reference between the models, and there is more possibility that a change will made in the conceptual model and propagated down. However, in practice this is rarely done.

The need for three models is more closely tied to the state of tooling and technology decades ago, rather than what is possible now. Applications can now be built directly on top of graph databases. The graph database makes it possible to have your cake and eat it too with regard to structure. The graph database, when combined with the new standard SHACL, allows application builders to define minimum structure that will be enforced. At the same time the inherent flexibility of the graph database, coupled with the open world assumptions of OWL, allows us to build models that have structure, but are not limited by that structure.

By using URIs as identifiers in the data model, once a concept has been defined (say in the equivalent of a conceptual model), the exact same URI is used in the equivalent of the logical and physical models. The logical conclusion is that the conceptual, logical, and physical are the same.

The real shift that needs to happen is a mental one. We've been separating conceptual, logical, and physical models for decades. We have a tendency to do conceptual modeling at a more abstract level, but this isn't necessary. If you start your conceptual core modeling project with "concrete abstractions," they can be used just as well in implementation as in design. Concrete abstractions are concepts that while they are at a more general level, can be implemented directly. The classes Person, Organization, Event, and Document fit this, as do properties such as hasPart, hasJurisdiction, governs, startDate or name.

SUMMARY

I hope that this book has suggested that the so-called "best practices" in implementing enterprise applications is anything but. Moreover, that you (as the sponsor of these systems) are being held hostage. Perhaps you (as the hostage-takers, if you have persevered), realize that the gig is up.

Hopefully, it is time for a new normal to emerge.

Frankly, the normal we have now is so bizarre that anything will be an improvement.

This change will have to be led by the buyers of systems, because the providers of systems have billions to gain by preserving the status quo and nothing to gain by improving things.

I hope that this book gives you enough to break the cycle of dependency.

To close the loop back to the first chapter: Lean manufacturing has made a religion the value of attacking waste at all its manifestations.

The Enterprise IT / Application Implementation Industries have waste at a level that would embarrass even the least lean of current manufacturers.

We hope this book is a call to arms. The cushy business as usual application implementation business is done. Million dollar projects with billion dollar prices tags are doomed.

It is time to begin curtailing projects that take us away from the naturally-integrated agile future. We must move toward an infrastructure that encourages reuse at every level and incremental improvement along the way, rather than "moon shots."

In the companion book, we outline a possible future. The Data Centric Revolution is not the only possible future, it is just an exemplar. We are putting it out there as an open standard so hopefully there will be many implementations. Many of you will be able to save yourselves hundreds of millions of dollars without even postulating what your end state will look like.

This book is about helping you out of the quagmire. The next book is an exemplar of what a post quagmire world might look like.

APPENDIX
Size of the Enterprise IT market

Surprisingly there does not seem to be a readily available source for the size of the Enterprise Information Technology industry. This is partly because of the way industry sizes are typically measured: each company is assigned a SIC (Standard Industrial Code) or NAICS (North American Industry Classification System) based on their primary activity. Because few firms are primarily in Enterprise IT, there isn't anything to roll up.

We will use two ways to triangulate into a reasonable figure for the total and then use some additional third party data to establish how much we should allocate to each factor of hardware, software licensing, networking, and professional services.

Per Euromonitor,[49] the world economy was nearly $70 trillion in 2016. Gartner estimated the average IT spend across all industries was 3.3% in 2014.[50] This gives us a figure of $2.3 trillion for the worldwide Enterprise IT market. Two other analyses give us comparable results.

Industry Segment	IT spending as a % of Revenue
Software Publishing and Internet Services	6.70%
Banking and Financial Services	6.30%
Media & Entertainment	5.00%
Education	4.70%
Professional Services	4.20%
Healthcare Providers	4.20%
Telecommunications	3.80%
Insurance	3.20%
Pharma, Life Science	3.20%
Utilities	2.80%
Transportation	2.60%
Industrial Electronics & Electrical Equip	2.50%
Consumer Products	1.90%
Industrial Manufacturing	1.70%
Retail & Wholesale	1.50%
Chemicals	1.30%
Food & Beverage Processing	1.30%
Energy	1.10%
Construction	1.00%
None	0.00%

---

[49] http://bit.ly/2BaHBvI.

[50] IT Key Metrics Data 2014, Gartner Benchmarks Analytics.

Taking a breakdown of the world economy by segment and multiplying by the above percentages gives us a surprisingly close $2.5 trillion. We suspect that Gartner's numbers are skewed to developed economies and particularly the United States. An alternative is to take an analysis done by Statista, which examined per capita IT spending by country. As suspected, there is about a 10:1 difference between the surveyed countries.

Country	Per Capita Spending on IT
USA	$3,356
UK	$2,754
Japan	$2,495
Germany	$2,040
France	$2,030
Italy	$1,284
Spain	$1,282
Brazil	$876
Russia	$557
China	$294

This is only 10 of the 200 countries in the world, but it gives us reference points. We assigned all the countries in the world to one of these categories. We assigned many populous countries such as Bangladesh and Ethiopia to a category that spends at 10% of the Chinese rate. This gave a total IT spend of $3.9 trillion.

Gartner separately has estimated the world IT spend at $3.8 trillion.[51]

---

[51] http://gtnr.it/2BJmqAJ.

Our four estimates gave us \$2.3, \$2.5, \$3.8, and \$3.9 trillion. We are going to accept Gartner's \$3.8 trillion for the rest of this analysis. This includes all spending (internal and external), hardware, and labor.

THE INDUSTRY BY FACTOR

In Chapter 2, we introduced the idea that the four primary factors of production for this industry are:

- **Hardware.** IDC report worldwide computer hardware spending to have been \$1.07 trillion in 2015.[52] We will assume that most of this, but not all was for Enterprise purposes. The PC hardware business is \$180 billion, some of which is B2C.
- **Networking.** Gartner reports that \$1.6 trillion of the \$3.8 trillion was spent on Telecom Services.[53]
- **Software Licenses.** Worldwide enterprise software spending is projected to be \$335 billion in 2015.[54]
- **Professional Services.** Gartner's figure for "IT services" is \$981 billion. It is not clear from this source whether that includes internal staff. The systems integration portion of the professional services industry is estimated to reach \$393 billion by 2020.[55]

---

[52] http://bit.ly/2kfv27T.

[53] http://gtnr.it/2BJmqAJ.

[54] http://gtnr.it/2BJmqAJ.

[55] http://bit.ly/2BuhInK.

Index

CPSIA information can be obtained
at www.ICGtesting.com
Printed in the USA
LVHW041052050119
602872LV00040B/1784/P

9 781634 623162